RELEASE

your

POTENTIAL

RELEASE
your
POTENTIAL

Using Your Gifts in a
Thriving Women's Ministry

ELIZABETH INRIG

MOODY PRESS
CHICAGO

All Scripture quotations, unless otherwise indicated, are taken from the *Holy Bible, New International Version*®. NIV®. Copyright © 1973, 1978, 1984 by International Bible Society. Used by permission of Zondervan Publishing House. All rights reserved.

Scripture quotations marked KJV are taken from the King James Version.

Scripture quotations marked NASB are taken from the *New American Standard Bible*®, © Copyright The Lockman Foundation 1960, 1962, 1963, 1968, 1971, 1972, 1973, 1975, 1977, 1995. Used by permission.

Library of Congress Catalogining-in-Piublication Data
Inrig, Elizabeth.
  Release your potential : using your gifts in a thriving women's ministry / Elizabeth Inrig.
    p. cm.
  Includes bibliographical references.
  ISBN 0-8024-8498-0
  1. Women clergy. I. Title.

BV676 .I57 2001
253'.082--dc21

                                                                    2001030519

                              1 3 5 7 9 10 8 6 4 2

                    Printed in the United States of America

To Gary,
whose passion for God's Word,
heart for God's glory,
and love for me
teaches me that ministry to women
is a holy entrustment from the Head of the church.

2 Corinthians 3:4–6
Such confidence as this is ours through Christ before God.
Not that we are competent in ourselves to claim anything for ourselves,
but our competence comes from God.
He has made us competent as ministers of a new covenant—not of the letter
but of the Spirit; for the letter kills, but the Spirit gives life.

CONTENTS

ACKNOWLEDGMENTS

$\mathcal{I}$n 1991 Greg Thornton of Moody Press flew to Dallas to have lunch with me and my husband. Greg asked me to consider writing a book related to women in ministry. I was, however, in the middle of a master's program at Dallas Seminary. I had also just come through a battle with breast cancer, and any extra time I had was spent teaching the Bible to women. It didn't seem to be the right time to write a book. I was content just putting roots deeply into the soil of God's Word. Ten years later, while I was finishing studies at another seminary and maintaining a local and national ministry to women, Greg asked me again to consider the task. The time was right and I thank God for the honor of sharing a ministry to women with Moody Press. *Release Your Potential* is the result.

As you read this book, you will learn how God surprised me when He led me to minister to women. So much of what I now do was not my idea! But as I look over my shoulder, I see more clearly how the Lord, the Head of the church, has orchestrated the details of my life. At every turn in my journey, He placed developing Christ followers in my path. They have shaped the vision I have for the local church, her spiritual health and tremendous potential as a place for women to serve.

Many people have influenced the way I follow Christ and the vision I have for women to serve women in the local church. My parents, now both with the Lord, instilled in me a deep reverence for Holy Scripture. They taught me to read it, learn it, and obey it, knowing it was the sole plumb line against which my life would someday be measured. Over the years, the writings of Elisabeth Elliot have helped me understand the importance of being a woman of God. I have been privileged to study in two fine theological seminaries. I thank God for the godly men who stirred in me the desire to dig more deeply into this amazing book called the Bible.

My most gracious teachers have been women in Canada, the United States, and other countries with whom I have sat with weekly to praise, to study, to pray, and to serve. To thank each one for the ways they cheered me along the journey would take more space than I have. But those who read this will remember exactly what God did during each stage of my life. I have a special place in my heart for those women in Winnipeg, Manitoba, who believed I could tell the story of Jesus to women who didn't know Him! I will forever be grateful to four elders' wives at Bethany Chapel in Calgary who believed I could and should teach a Bible study in the context of the local church. They taught me the wisdom of working as a team so we could all use our spiritual gifts. I am thankful too to the ladies at Reinhardt Bible Church in Dallas who entrusted to me the responsibility of overseeing the Bible study program. The lessons I learned in leadership were indispensable.

To the elders and pastoral staff at Trinity Church in Redlands, California, I can only say: "I thank God upon every remembrance of you." Your faithful prayer and joyful partnership in this ministry to women enables me to serve wholeheartedly at Trinity as well as in the Evangelical Free Church of America. Words are not adequate to express my love and thanks to the women at Trinity church who partner with me in so many ways. Thank you for modeling hearts that are open to God's Word and hands that willingly serve women. To the women's ministry team of the Evangelical Free Church of America, with whom I have had the honor of serving as National Director, God be praised for the way you have partnered in the vision we have for growing godly women for the common good of the church.

For more than thirty-five years I have sat under my husband Gary's consistent teaching of God's Word. He has urged me to serve the Lord and freed me for many hours of studying and writing. He, with our children Janice, Stephen, and Heather and their life-partners, has cheered me on to run this race with diligence. Thank you for all your encouraging words along the way.

With joy on the journey and all glory to Jesus.
ELIZABETH INRIG
Redlands, California

INTRODUCTION

*I*n the closing minutes of the last day of 1981, I learned in a new way the value of having known a godly woman. Our children were in bed. My husband was in Dallas finishing doctoral work at Dallas Seminary. The flames chased around the fireplace in our Calgary home like the thoughts in my head. My father's earlier phone call saddened me. "Your mother's breast cancer has spread to her liver. She is starting chemotherapy."

On KMBI, the Moody Bible Institute station we cabled in from Spokane, Washington, *Songs in the Night* was playing its last song of the old year. The words caught my attention. "Whatever it takes to draw closer to You, Lord, that's what I'll be willing to do."

I fell to my knees to do what hosts of Christ followers had done before me: *I gave up control of life's circumstances one more time to the only One who can be trusted with it. And I thanked the Lord for giving me a godly mother.* Less than three months later my mother died, but not before I had time to thank her for modeling truth on how to live with wisdom *and* how to die with grace. Her life had affected me for my good and God's glory. What she did for me, she had done for other women as well, not as part of a program or an event with an agenda, but as a lifestyle in obedience to God's Word. She was a godly woman. That moment of stillness gave me a chance to appreciate the priceless value of having a godly woman affect one's life. This book celebrates the potential blessing for the local church when godly women serve women.

Like many Christian women, I never planned to work with women. I was a schoolteacher. As a newly married seminary wife, I understood very little of organized women's ministries. I resisted the idea that such a thing should define the pattern of my life. But over the years I began to meet women who knew God well, women who valued ministering to women. These women modeled a godly grace I loved to be around. Many have affected my life forever. Many more continue to use their gifts to grow godly women for the spiritual health of the local church. This book reflects what I believe God can do in the local churches of our land when godly women are released to reach their spiritual potential. It is written with the conviction that your local church has the potential for spiritual health when godly women are freed to minister to women. It shows how God intends the local church to function like a family. It is not about programs; we all have more than we can handle. It is not about seminars or things to keep women busy. It is an appeal to women who believe in the value God places on women to take a fresh look at God's holy Word. It comes with the hope that when women who desire to be godly freely embrace God's eternal purposes for their lives, they keep the church family spiritually healthy and enjoy a thriving women's ministry.

Three influential people have shaped my understanding of God's plan for women to minister in the body of Christ. The first was my mother. She modeled ministry to women in a time when there were few paradigms to follow. She prayed with and taught God's Word to women in her church, one woman at a time. She modeled deeds of kindness and faithfully explained the gospel to those who did not know the Lord Jesus. The second influence is the group of godly women friends who have taught me how to live wisely, who love God's Word, who willingly trust His heart even when they may not understand His ways. They pray, they love God, they seek truth, and each one mentored and nurtured me toward godliness. They continue to show me how to have a long story of walking with God.

But it is the man whom God brought into my life and whom I married in 1966, who helped me see the potential for women's ministries. For all these years, my husband, Gary, has urged me to move beyond my comfort zone to serve the Lord Jesus. He saw beyond my fears and urged me as a young wife and mother to see opportunities to serve women as "entrustments" from God instead of "intrusions." He models Paul's description of love in 1 Corinthians 13. He encourages me to use my gifts in the context of the local church for the good of women, for the health of the local church, and for the glory of God. Because of his encouragement, I have had the holy privilege of ministering to women for more than thirty years.

This book reflects things I have learned along the way. The words are for believers who care about the spiritual health of their local church. They are for women who call themselves "Christ followers" and long to see women in their believing community *become fully developed Christ followers*. The words are for those who minister in the context of the local church. They are a call to men and women who lead our churches to exercise a new godliness and sensitivity as they uphold the complementary nature of roles in God's family. They include an attempt to persuade Christian women not to create ministry in a vacuum but to serve Christ, using their gifts as equal partners in the local church so that, together with men, they can take hold of this holy calling with great celebration. The quotes used at the beginning of each chapter have been gathered from women in North America and other continents. They are written by women who live their lives as Christ followers in the marketplace, in the home, and in the local church. In most cases I do not know the name of the woman who made the comment in a seminar or workshop setting, but where I know who said it, I have provided her name.

As you consider the spiritual potential of the women in *your* church, do not dismiss God's particular calling to women as ancient and irrelevant. Instead, as you read this book, come back with me to the basics of Scripture, to the grand revelation of the holy mystery of God's purposes for the church before time began. Rejoice in your God-given responsibility of ministering to women. Help men in your church promote a new respect for God's purposes for women in your local church, valuing highly those who are godly. As a church, in a day when women and some men value the advice of Dr. Laura, Oprah Winfrey, and Judge Judy over the inspired Word of God, I appeal to you to seek above all things to practice the principles of Scripture in a fresh and freeing way. When you do, you, with me, will discover God's Word to be true: The watching world around us will not "malign the word of God" (Titus 2:5).

Chapter One

FAMILY
MATTERS

"It matters to women that women are in their lives. It should matter to me since I am a woman!"

"The girls need to be with the girls!"

GIG KAVALICH

"Every church family needs women who will take the 'woman to woman moment' any time of the day."

"If the Lord leaves us here on earth for a little longer, the future generations need to be taught, led, challenged to use their gifts to serve God. Whatever your age, the women of today are responsible to make this happen!"

"Women have a common bond and that bond helps when ministering to one another. It is a good place to start because by being a woman you already have things in common with at least half the family!"

LAURA HOOD

"Likewise, teach the older women to be reverent in the way they live, not to be slanderers or addicted to much wine, but to teach what is good. Then they can train the younger women to love their husbands and children, to be self-controlled and pure, to be busy at home, to be kind, and to be subject to their husbands, so that no one will malign the word of God."

Titus 2:3–5

FAMILY MATTERS

*B*efore I agreed to marry my husband, Gary, I had already said I wouldn't marry a preacher or a missionary. It wasn't that I didn't like preachers; I just wasn't sure what they did with their time! I was afraid to marry a missionary because I wasn't sure how missionaries paid their bills. (I have since learned that this can be true for any person on a budget.)

Before I understood how carefully God prepares our path and leads us in His ways, I said a lot of other "never's." I had a lot to learn about trusting the Lord Jesus for everyday life. You may have even made the kind of statements I made: "I'll never leave my mother, I'll never leave Vancouver, I'll never stand up in front of women, I'll never move to the Canadian prairies, I'll never move to Dallas again, and one thing is certain: We'll never live in California!"

The words may sound silly to you, but the truth behind them made sense to me: *Family matters to me.* And the family that mattered all lived on the West Coast. As my love for Gary grew and my understanding of God's mysterious ways of guiding His children strengthened (Proverbs 3:5–6), I began to trust His heart even when I did not understand His ways.

This book reflects what I believe God is looking for in the church today: godly women who are willing to fulfill the eternal purposes of God by ministering to women and so enabling the church to be spiritually healthy.

There has never been a time in the history of man when the idea of womanhood draws more opinions from people around the globe. The postmodern world offers women a smorgasbord of options, all clamoring for attention. In a way like never before, the church of Jesus Christ tries to define what a woman is, could be, or should be.

The serious Christ follower who has straddled a few decades knows the importance of staying focused on the eternal purposes of God. She cares about His purposes because she knows they are bigger than her personal plans. She recognizes that God's purposes are grander than any programs created by the human mind. She is convinced that God's purposes for Christian women make the arrogance of a rebellious culture fade into the dust. Whether the Old Testament: "In his heart a man plans his course, but the LORD determines his steps" (Proverbs 16:9) or the New: "And we know that in all things God works for the good of those who love him, who have been called according to his purpose" (Romans 8:28), you will find God carefully working out His purposes in the world. Nothing any one of us can dream up will change the Father's eternal purpose to call us to honor His Son: "Therefore God exalted him to the highest place and gave him the name that is above every name, that at the name of Jesus every knee should bow, in heaven and on earth and under the earth, and every tongue confess that Jesus Christ is Lord, to the glory of God the Father" (Philippians 2:9–11). Paul says God's primary tool through which He works today is His church family (Ephesians 3:10).

That was the part that was missing in my equation: The family that matters to women must include the local family of God. The God of the Bible looks at the concept of "family" with the panoramic lens of the camera. He was not bothered that I moved away from my family of human origin so much as He wanted me to open my heart to the church family. He had spiritual mothers and fathers, brothers and sisters I needed to meet so they would help me grow up as a Christian woman. I found myself repeating the words of the Lord Jesus Himself: "If anyone comes to me and does not hate his father and mother, his wife and children, his brothers and sisters— yes, even his own life—he cannot be my disciple" (Luke 14:26).

As Christ followers, we must come to grips with discipleship. We cannot follow the Savior without giving up our lives. We cannot fulfill God's purposes without being intimately connected to His church, the local expression of His body. This means I am never apart from the family. When I married a preacher and moved away from my human family, I made that marvelous discovery. God's family shows up everywhere, in towns and cities around the world. They cluster together in groups and, regardless of their size, God's intention is that they reflect His eternal purposes. God's purposes for the church are similar to those of the human family: It's where people learn to grow up and show off the glory of God! For our purposes, it is where women can learn to become fully developed Christ followers.

LESSONS FROM THE FAMILY

The purpose of this book is to convince you that as a woman, *you are essential to your local church's spiritual health.* Since the local church is the supernatural womb where baby Christ followers are nurtured, you are a spiritual mother. The local church is the nursery in which Christian toddlers are trained and the home where God's children of all ages are discipled to maturity. You need to be part of that process. Since at least half the members in any local church are women, as Christian women of this generation, it is essential for you to understand your part in God's purposes for His family. When women use their gifts to minister to women, the church grows in spiritual health; women achieve their God-given potential and His purposes.

What Women Value in God's Family

When our children were young, our family traveled across the United States and Canada to family camps where my husband would speak and we would be together as a family. One of our favorite pastimes on the way was pulling out memories from the past. It was a way we could walk down memory lane, discussing names, events, treasures, favorite times, or teachers whose lives influenced us for good. We appreciated honoring people who helped us understand what it meant to be grown up.

Each woman I have ever met has stories, memories from the past of women whom God has used to influence her for good. As women tell me what these women have done to help them achieve their God-given potential, I encourage them to write a note of thanks for what the person means to them. If you were to write such a list, it might include a mother, an aunt, or a teacher. You may remember someone who was in your life for a single moment or has been with you for a lifetime.

In a thousand responses, some of the things women value about these influencers are interesting to me. Because *women want to be understood,* they said they valued those who listened to them. They said they valued those who *knew and used their name* as well as those who *missed them when they were gone* and kept in touch with them. But most of all, the kind of woman valued most was the one who *modeled an authentic relationship with God.*

The challenge of growing in Christ so we influence other women for good in the churches in which we meet is no less important now than it was when women first followed Jesus and served in the early church. The questions still need to be asked: How can the church release the spiritual potential intrinsic in her women? What kind of woman is God looking for, and how can she influence others for good? What steps does the church take when it seeks to urge women to use their gifts for the good of the Christian family and the glory of God? What kind of woman does the church need in this generation? Why should women minister to women in the context of the local church?

Unless these questions are answered on the basis of the eternal written Word of God, the spiritual health of the local church is in jeopardy. The promise of a new generation of godly women is at stake.

What God Values in His Church

God values women who are committed to becoming fully developed Christ followers. To be devoted to Christ is the beginning. To become a fully developed Christ follower is to know what God values in His church, why He values it, and how He loves to see it portrayed before a watching world. We discover when we read His Word that He praises women like Mary, the young teen who submitted to His will without knowing everything there is to know. We see Him welcome a woman like the Samaritan, whom the disciples would have ignored had *they* wanted a drink. We see Him ministered to by wealthy women of Herod's court as they traverse Palestine with Him and His disciples. We hear His delight with women like Mary of Bethany, who sits quietly at His side listening to His heart and are so glad He protects her from the anger of Judas and the rest when, at the right time, she unselfishly pours out her treasure on Him. He values single women who are passionate for His glory. He respects married women who uphold the honor of marriage and mothering. And after His return to heaven, His apostles continued His high regard for women in the early church. We know He is pleased when women like John Mark's mother open their homes to the church family. We read of women using all kinds of gifts, whether a businesswoman like Lydia, a theological thinker like Priscilla, or a domestic woman like Phoebe.

Because women are behind the scenes at every turn in the growth of the New Testament church, we come to a single conclusion: What God values, we must value. We must not value one woman over another because she is our kind or fits in with a particular group the way we think important. We must value every woman who belongs to the Savior, recognizing that God is pleased when she fulfills His purpose in the church.

EMBRACING THE PLAN

To ignore His plan for our lives is to refuse His blessing upon us. As we reexamine the Scriptures, we will discover that God is less concerned about tradition for its own sake than we are, unless the tradition constitutes a command. He is more concerned that women in God's family experience personal transformation. He is also not as impressed with the new programs or novel implementations as we are. He is more concerned that *we know Him through His Word so we may obey His will.* His words to Martha remain the same to us: Stop worrying about how many things you need to cook or serve. Mary is listening to Me, and she has chosen the better part (Luke 10:38–42).

DETERMINING FACTORS FOR WOMEN'S MINISTRIES

Where you live, your age as a Christ follower, the stage of your life, the size of your church, or the nature of your spiritual gift is not the determining factor for the Christian life or women's ministries. The determining factor is this: the present health of your spiritual relationship with the Lord Jesus Christ. Are you more committed to doing what you have always done than you are to spiritually growing up? Are you more focused on doing Christian events than living a corporate or personal godly lifestyle? Are you living with joy in the local church family in which God has put you? How concerned are you about the spiritual health of your brothers and sisters in Christ who meet with you weekly in Christian community? If the spiritual health of the women in your church depended on your commitment, how healthy would your church be? These are the questions to ask if you would become a woman who ministers to the members of the body as God intends you to do: for the good of the whole family and the glory of God.

STARTING OUT

Most of us do not know what we are doing when we begin to serve the Lord Jesus except that we are seeking to obey Him. We may have had a friend or family member teach us some basic life principles, but very few of us ever start with everything in place. We know we love Him. We know we want to be known as His disciples. But for the most part, just as in our human childhood, we learn as we go. We learn by doing, by serving, by following. So it is only right to ask the questions: When and where do we begin in order to see a ministry to women thrive and grow? At the outset of this book, let me suggest some things I have had to learn as a reluctant servant.

Begin Where You Are

You have been placed in your family and a specific local church by the providential working of God. Whether you are part of an organized women's ministry in your local church or are simply committed to ministering to women in your church, you are called to be a spiritual leader. A leader is simply someone who influences another person for good. With leadership or influence comes the ability to effect change in others. Influencing others for their spiritual good may include the ability to cast a vision for what women can do. Influence is able to convince others of the value of the vision. It is the ability to motivate a team to achieve the purpose of the vision so they finally embrace the vision themselves. It is doing what Moses did when God called him. Though he was reluctant, God taught him to begin where he was. He had to take him from the desert to Egypt, but when Moses got there and God convinced him He would go with him, he was all there. Oh, there was a fairly heated discussion about who would be the leader, but once Moses realized *who* had called him, he stopped his arguing and won this epitaph from the writer to the Hebrews: "Moses was faithful as a servant in all God's house" (Hebrews 3:5).

Go with the Goers and Pray-ers

Do not wait for the big plan. Do not strategize or scheme for something you can't possibly do. Begin where you are with the women God has placed in your life. Begin by praying with another one or two women who really believe God answers prayer and blesses obedience. As you read God's Word, pray together for Him to lead you.

Many years ago, I learned this firsthand in Calgary when the churches in our city hosted a Billy Graham crusade. Our third child had just begun kindergarten. I found I had a few hours of discretionary time besides the time given to my Bible study group. So I became the prayer chairman for the crusade. I planned a prayer rally. Hundreds of women came to the rally. I announced at the rally our plans for prayer groups around the city, and many women were motivated to pray. One hundred invitations went out asking women to join me at my home for prayer. I was a little nervous wondering what would happen were everyone to come to our home.

I didn't need to worry! When the day came for the prayer time, three ladies came to my house. I was annoyed. "If I can't get women to pray for Billy Graham, who in the world would they pray for?"

I carried my irritation with me to the meeting Charlie Riggs led for the follow-up volunteers at the Graham crusades. I will never forget his challenging words after I whined about my disappointment. He told me, "Elizabeth, go with the goers." He defined the goers. "The women who got in the car and came to your house to pray are the goers!" Then he quoted James 5:16b, "The prayer of a righteous man is powerful and effective." We prayed for many weeks together and saw God answer our prayers.

Similar scenes have been true for me over the years in women's ministries. A few show up to study God's Word or pray or serve. They are the "goers." They are those who count on God's faithfulness. They will be among those who are faithful to God in small things when no one but God is looking. Those who are faithful in the small things can be trusted with greater things. Always go with the goers, the pray-ers.

Begin with a Plan

Repeatedly throughout Scripture, God is said to work according to eternal purposes (Ephesians 3:10–11). He does not act without a plan. Nor should we! The Lord Jesus did His earthly work based on a team of followers, sometimes three, other times twelve, sometimes as many as seventy-two. For a thriving women's ministry to work, plans need to be made on two levels: the personal level and the partnership level.

As a woman of influence—and every woman who calls herself a Christ follower influences someone—you will never get beyond the need to have a personal plan for godliness. You will need to do the following well.

- Take care of your own soul first. (Psalm 1:1–3; Proverbs 4:23; 1 Timothy 6:20)
- Think biblically about influence and leadership: It is a call to servanthood. The Lord's approval is the primary goal. (2 Timothy 4:6–7)
- Know why you are doing what you are doing. Purposes are bigger than plans, and God's purposes are the grandest of all! (Proverbs 16:3–4; Romans 12:1–2)

- Resolve to be congruent where your inside thoughts and attitudes match your behaviors and choices. (1 Thessalonians 2:5–12)
- Choose to be proactive rather than reactive, knowing that at the end of the day you will give an account not to your mother, your father, your husband, or a good friend. You will give an account to the Lord for the resources He has put in your hand. (1 Thessalonians 2:4; 1 Corinthians 3:10–15)

Partner with Others

When you partner with others to grow a thriving women's ministry, there may be a tendency to think that if positions get filled, then the job will get done. A careful look at leadership or influence confirms that thriving women's ministries require a team of women who commit to develop people over positions, who share a partnership rather than programs, and who view women's ministry as a lifestyle rather than an event. They apply principles from God's Word to present needs. They value the process of coming alongside one another as a team, working from the roots up instead of the top down. Regardless of the size of your church or the stage of your women's ministries, you will need to partner with others in a plan.

The first step is always to seek the Lord together. Look for women whose heart He has prepared and begin to pray—together. Pray the prayers of Scripture, pray without ceasing, pray at all times, pray on your own, and set time aside to pray together. It is in the context of prayer and the Word that we come to know God's heart and understand His ways. He wants to be involved in your planning.

People are the essential asset in building a team. Get to know the women in your local church who possess personal godly character and are already involved in other women's lives in a godly manner. You are not looking for warm bodies to fill a space. You are seeking others who share your love for God, His will, and His ways and who care for women. Pray with these people asking God to lead you where He is already working.

The key to being a team player requires the ability to work with women different from yourself. To build a team you will need three kinds of people:

A visionary—a woman who *sees where you need to go*
A shepherd—a woman who *takes care of you as you go*
An administrator—a woman who *gets you where you need to go*

Expect Prepared People

Willing people are not enough. Look for those whom God has prepared in different ways through previous life experiences. Look for those who model faithful service in the church. The wise woman finds others prepared by God who can do things she could never do so she can do what God wants her to do. Influencers are good leaders whom God has prepared because they have first been good followers.

Because you have prayed for God to lead you to prepared individuals, you will be amazed how God goes ahead in so many ways. When you ask women to join in serving who are prepared by God, they do not give you the answer, "Let me pray about it for a month!" That is too long to wait if God has already been working in a person's heart. Sometimes a person might say, "Let me pray about it" when she really means, "I don't want to." Press for the reason she can't give you an answer today, and set a date by which you will get an answer from her. For extra study in two kinds of responses to God's call, check out the story of Moses (see Exodus 3 and 4:13–17) and the story of Mary (Luke 1:26–38).

God's Word is clear about His solution to anxiety and worry. It is prayer. The result of Spirit-directed prayer is peace. Any prayerful strategy that God blesses comes with a sense of peace as the Lord assures you that the decisions and directions are from Him. The promise that the Holy Spirit intercedes even when we don't know what to say should give us the quiet assurance of divine peace.

WOMEN WHO WEAR THE FRAGRANCE OF CHRIST

One of the influencers in my life is a New Zealander named J. Oswald Sanders. I have listened to Mr. Sanders by tape on the topic of discipleship hundreds of times. His books on leadership and discipleship are among the best I have read. A favorite story of mine that Sanders tells is about an experiment he did for a Bible college class in Auckland. To teach them the importance of Christian influence on other people's lives, he asked a young woman from another class to come and walk through the class saying nothing. After she had gone, Sanders asked his class if they had noticed anything.

"Anything at all?"

A few said they noticed a woman had walked through the room. Some commented on the length of her hair, the color of her dress. Another noted she had said nothing; she just came and then she was gone.

"Anything else?" Sanders pressed the class for another answer.

They could not think of anything unusual until finally one of the young students said, "Her fragrance. Yes, I noticed she was wearing a beautiful fragrance, a lovely perfume."

"That's it! That's influence. The fragrance of your life speaks even when you say nothing."

Mr. Sanders turned the class to Paul's discussion of the new covenant where he says, "Thanks be to God, who always leads us in triumphal procession in Christ and through us spreads everywhere the fragrance of the knowledge of him. For we are to God the aroma of Christ among those who are being saved" (2 Corinthians 2:14–15).

The secret to releasing your potential in the local church begins with you. The way to grow a thriving women's ministry has everything to do with the fragrance you choose to wear. Every woman who becomes a godly influencer among women wears the fragrance of Christ. It comes as a result of spending time with Him. Like Mary of Bethany after she poured out her treasured nard on the Savior (John 12:1–8), the fragrance of His character is all over us and evident to those we meet.

Great abilities do not make you useful to God. Nor do programs you arrange or performances you give because of your gifts. The ministry to women that God blesses depends on women who resolve to bear great likeness to the Savior. Does your church wish to release the spiritual potential among women? Count on God to do for you what you can never do for yourself. Do you want to invest for eternity? See your ministry women as an entrustment from Him, not an intrusion. Do you want a thriving ministry in your local church among women? Make your walk with God the priority relationship in your life, and God, whose eyes range throughout the earth, will strengthen your heart as it is fully committed to Him (2 Chronicles 16:9a). Count on Him for today, and He will establish your tomorrows.

THINK IT OVER

1. Have you been reluctant to serve women in the context of your local church? Why?

2. What in your life does God use as a means for you to serve women in your local church?

3. Who in your church shares a similar concern for women's ministries?

4. If you could change one thing about the ministry to women in your church, what would it be? Why?

5. What one solution would you bring to help grow a thriving women's ministry in your local church?

6. With whom do you pray on a regular basis for women or the women's ministry in your church? What do you pray? How has God answered those prayers?

THINK IT THROUGH

Take some time and think about the way the following women served in the local church.

1. Tabitha/Dorcas	Acts 9:36–43
2. Mary, John's mother	Acts 12:5–19
3. Lydia	Acts 16:13–15, 40
4. Priscilla	Acts 18:18, 24–26; Romans 16:3–5
5. Other women	Romans 16:6, 12

LESSONS FROM THE FAMILY

"As an older woman, the reason I believe women should minister to women is simple: The Bible says that is how the family of God works best. Like the human family, women are asked to nurture younger women in the church, caring for them and teaching them what is good for the good of the generations after us! I can do that!"

ANN TOLERICO, Bible Study Leader

"Women should take seriously caring for each other in God's family because there is a chronic shortage of the Titus 'older women' who are approachable and available."

"My mother loved, feared, and served God; she was never ashamed to show the passion and devotion to the Lord Jesus and the church family we were a part of. She repeatedly put others before herself and wanted us to understand how gracious God was."

"My paternal aunt took me as a three-month-old baby, during wartime. It took me years to understand that most people thought it was a 'snag' to have an 'Aunty Meg' instead of a 'Mum.' I certainly didn't lack for any love or mothering. Aunty Meg took me to church and taught me to love Jesus in a church that missed the meaning of His sacrifice. Aunty Meg led me to give my heart to Him so He could then come and find me after I had strayed. She taught me to put my faith in Him."

AUSTRALIAN FRIEND

"My 'adopted' mother was the daughter of missionary parents in Iran. She loved the Lord Jesus and she loved me! More than that, she taught me to love the family of God."

Chapter Two

LESSONS FROM THE FAMILY

*T*he hospital says we can have one other person in the birthing room. We want you."

I was both flattered and nervous. Not medical in my thinking, I marveled at this option given to our daughters compared to my experience thirty years earlier. My husband had been banished to the waiting room for the births of our first two children. He witnessed only the birth of our third child.

"Don't you want to be there when the baby is delivered?"

Secretly, I knew I didn't have a choice. Both girls wanted me present with their husbands to share in their event. They wanted their father discreetly nearby. So we did what they wanted us to do. In the early stages of labor, we waited together, preparing the mother-to-be by serving her needs in any way we could. For me, it meant serving like a "doula," caring for each of my daughters in tangible ways: a warm bath, drinks of cold water, gentle touches, and nourishing foods to meet the need of the moment. The moment the hard labor started, I joined in coaching each one toward the goal: the safe delivery of a healthy human baby. With each of our sons-in-law, it meant experiencing the miracle of life.

BIRTH IS ALWAYS AMAZING

I was not prepared for the impact witnessing the births of my grand-children had on me. To behold the wonder of new life is a powerful experience. To watch two healthy babies join our family, amid the pain and push of the laboring mother, leaves me in awe of God. Each baby's scream shouted to me "God is the source of life!" The hungry cries for milk from the mother's breast only made me praise God's wisdom. Who but the God of Scripture could draw the plans for something as amazing as the female body? Only He could design a way to provide for the ongoing growth and maturity of little ones.

Neither the little girl nor the little boy, arriving on the doorstep of our family fourteen months apart, knew anything of their history. They didn't know how their parents met, the influence their grandparents had had on the way their mothers and fathers would bring them up. They didn't know how their future would be shaped, or how our family worked, played, or prayed together. They were unaware of the heart language of our family. It was enough to know they were alive and had taken their first breath. We in the family knew they had come at the appointed time in the order of life's events: There is a "time to be born . . ." (Ecclesiastes 3:2). Now we had a new responsibility together as a family to these little ones: to equip them to live as fully developed human beings. I left the birthing rooms convinced that it is God who shapes the human heart to nurture and be nurtured. It is He who creates the human breast to nourish a hungry child. It is His design that hungry babies not stay infants but grow to maturity.

Lessons from the Human Family

What God has planned for us in the physical and relational realm He intends for us in the spiritual realm. The mystery of how this happens is shown in the context of the new organism He birthed on Pentecost called the church. Like a metaphor teaching the truth, the human family is the basis on which we understand how to behave in God's forever family. Paul describes it in Ephesians 4:15 where he says the goal of being part of the body of Christ is that we would "grow up into him who is the Head, that is, Christ." It is from Christ that the whole family of God is birthed. As each individual part of the body does its work, each one grows up to maturity. It is for this reason that the human family becomes our primary pattern or paradigm for what it means to grow up spiritually. Just witnessing the birth of two grandchildren makes the lesson abundantly clear.

A Healthy Birthing Body

A healthy body is a priority for birthing a healthy baby. Each daughter had tried to prepare her body carefully for the moment of birth. Both of them watched what they ate, determined to invest in the health of the baby. They exercised. They rested. They refused to drink caffeine. They did everything they could to ensure a safe delivery, a strong baby.

If you know the Lord Jesus Christ personally, you have been birthed by the Holy Spirit of God. If you have received eternal life, it is because God has made you alive by the work of His Spirit (John 3:6). On the day of your new birth, you had little understanding of the family of God into which you were coming. It was enough to know that you had been born of God, brought to a safe spiritual delivery by the Spirit.

The Presence of Wise Counsel

As soon as our daughters knew they were pregnant, each one looked for wisdom from women who had already given birth. Although the Internet supplied them with more information on every aspect of pregnancy than they could take in, they favored spending time with friends. They learned from other women who had delivered babies. They realized they were not the first to have a baby. They valued women who had coached other women through countless births. They were better prepared for childbirth than I had been when I gave birth to them, decades earlier. As they continue the challenging job of parenting, we as the grandparents encourage and support them in every way we can. We've been there. We know the importance of a support system.

Even if you have never birthed a human child or become a grandparent, as a member of the community of Christians you know the importance of others coming alongside you in support and in comfort. One of the most wonderful things in the family of God is the fact that all of us have spiritual parents God puts in our life. They come in all shapes and sizes. Some are birth parents to us, and others are serendipitously put in our lives by God's providence. All have proved God's ways of wisdom. One or two become models, mentors, and disciplers who encourage us to walk the journey to the end. These family members who have been walking with God longer than we have are indispensable to our spiritual growth.

The Importance of Extended Family

For many years, my friends who became grandparents before me used to haul out the pictures of their grandbabies. I'd be thinking, "Get a life!" as I smiled and looked at the baby pictures. They all looked pretty much the same to me, just one more member of the human race. But now I'm a grandmother. Everything is different. It's not just that I now care about pictures (I have my own set!), but I care about the lives of these children. And it matters to me that my immediate family and good friends value our grandchildren. I love that they love them. I appreciate when they ask about them. I'm honored when they want to know how they're doing, if they're sleeping through the night, what new things they can do, if they can say "Grammy" yet. I am overwhelmed with their love for my children and grandchildren. Just now, the little ones are oblivious to the importance of the care of this network of relationships. But as they grow up, they will learn they have history. They will learn how important it is that they have links of relationships to real people to whom their existence matters.

The same thing is wonderfully true for all Christ followers. When you come into the Christian family, you come to a whole extended family, a whole community. You come to a family whose roots go back to ancient days (Galatians 3:7). You come to a community whose history is written in the eternal letters of the New Testament. You find you have a "great cloud of witnesses" (Hebrews 12:1) who model faith, have finished the journey well, and are cheering you on to maturity and endurance.

When you come into the Christian family, you discover you have come into a spiritual family whose relatives span the globe. Because we have come to Christ, "the living Stone," we are what Peter calls "living stones, . . . being built into a spiritual house" (1 Peter 2:4–5). We are members of the universal church composed of all believers in the Lord Jesus Christ. More important, as a birthed and growing Christ follower, you discover you have a spiritual family composed of Christ's children right in your local community. You have the joy of being part of a local church of Jesus Christ. It is in the local church that the family lives out its life together. It is in the local family of Christians that we share a common life with brothers and sisters, that we learn from mothers and fathers under the Headship of the Lord Jesus. It is in the local church that we begin to love family members who have gifts we need in order to grow up. And we discover that because they love our Lord, they love us, too!

The local church of which you are a part is the primary place you show how well you get along with the Christian family. It is the natural nursery where spiritual babies are born and the children of God develop (1 Peter 2:1–3). To help us understand this, Paul uses the word *ekklesia* to describe the local congregation or assembly of believers (1 Corinthians 3:16–17). It is in the context of the local church that grown Christians model maturity (Christlikeness) and young Christians are taught to obey. It is in the context of the local church that Christ followers prove they can get along together as a unified family in spite of their diversity. Paul helps us see the way it was meant to be by using a picture of the human body. In Romans 12:4–5, he says: "Just as each of us has one body with many members, and these members do not all have the same function, so in Christ we who are many form one body, and each member belongs to all the others."

In his letter to the church at Philippi, he says the most important thing they will ever do to prove they have met Jesus Christ is *to be like-minded and take care of each other.* In the family of God, they will need to "in humility consider others better than [them]selves" (Philippians 2:1–4).

FULLY DEVELOPED FOLLOWERS OF CHRIST

The effect on the members of a human family who live, serve, and care for each other is they experience personal growth as individuals and as a group. That's what is happening with our grandchildren. They are growing and, for their age, they are getting along well in our family. They are doing all the things little humans do. And if you ask their parents what they hope for them, they will say they are having a measure of success in teaching them to obey, how to eat, how to speak, and how to get along in the family. And when they finally grow up, the parents will agree as hordes of parents before them, "We have brought them up to be mature adults who have the potential to be *fully developed human beings!*"

At the end of the day it won't matter to God the size of our church, the number of its programs, or the multiple services or choices we made available to others. What will matter will be that the Father's eternal purposes were accomplished in our lives. What will matter to Him is whether we became *fully developed Christ followers.* In the same way we seek to eat food, get enough rest, and exercise for good physical health, so God has provided for our spiritual health in every way. He longs that we would not be satisfied acting like children playing in mud puddles when we can spend our life drinking in the clear, cool waters of His Word. Perhaps the best description of God's purpose for His children is given in Colossians 1:28–29 where Paul describes his own heart for those he serves. "We proclaim him, admonishing and teaching everyone with all wisdom, so that we may present everyone perfect [mature, grown up] in Christ. To this end I labor, struggling with all his energy, which so powerfully works in me." It is this greater purpose we need to adopt for the family of God if we would be women who nurture and nourish women in our local church.

God is looking for fully developed Christ followers. He is concerned about transformation from infancy to adulthood. He is not as impressed with the new and the novel as we are, unless it plants seeds for eternity. He is more concerned that we obey Him and love the family into which

He has placed us. Where you live, the stage of your life, the size of your church, or the nature of your spiritual gift is not the determining factor for your Christian life. The determining factor is how committed are you to growing up? How focused are you on the local church family in which God has placed you? How concerned are you about the spiritual health of your brothers and sisters in Christ? Those are the questions to ask if you would become a woman who ministers to the members of the body as God intends you to do: for the good of the whole family and the glory of God.

How the Family of God Works

I have chosen to develop this book with a discourse on babies coming into a family with a purpose: As I minister to women in a variety of churches, I see the analogy of the human family and the church family being played out. When all the family members of a local church understand God's high intention for every member of the family to become a fully developed Christ follower, the church is healthy. When the growing of godly women is a core value in a church, healthy conditions are set for women to minister effectively to women. Church leaders who value this holy calling for women empower the local church to reflect the glory of God in the community and the universe as declared by Paul in Ephesians 3:10–11: "His intent was that now, through the church, the manifold wisdom of God should be made known to the rulers and authorities in the heavenly realms, according to his eternal purpose which he accomplished in Christ Jesus our Lord."

Like good parents in a family, churches that share the Spirit's purpose to grow *fully developed Christ followers* commit to at least four things.

1. They seek to *provide spiritual food* for every member, appropriate to age and stage.
2. They *promote an atmosphere* that grows healthy spiritual relationships within the church family and motivates believers to seek people not yet in the family.
3. They *shelter the church family* from unnecessary activities that waste their resources and harmful influences that endanger their well-being.
4. They *advocate and model personal spiritual disciplines* whereby the family members learn not only to begin but to finish their spiritual journeys well.

The Task Before Us

The task of this book is to answer the question, *"Why should women minister to women in the context of the local church?"* To answer that question, some assumptions should be stated.

We will *take Scripture seriously,* knowing that God as Creator of the human family is Creator of the believing family. Just as He has specific purposes for men and women in the human family, so He has in His Christian family.

We will *seek to follow the pattern of the church family that pleases God* as carefully as we follow the pattern for the human family. When we honor God's Word and obey His ways, we please God.

We will *value the history of the church as pictured in Acts,* thereby understanding how the Holy Spirit births the church and each individual believer.

We will *take our instructions from the apostle Paul's letters,* as the worthy model of how the church, led by Christ her Head, should live in any generation. In doing this, we will understand how principles in the Epistles speak afresh to the issue of women's ministries in the local church.

My Passion and Prayer for Women of This Generation

Many years ago I was involved in a wives' fellowship class for student wives at Dallas Seminary. The first hour was taught by seminary professors, the second by their wives. Sitting in the audience at Chafer Chapel, we were a mixed group from all over the world. Most of us were newlyweds, except for the women who spoke to us the second hour. I was impressed by these godly men and women who invested their lives in women soon to be ministry-wives. It was during these evenings so long ago that I came to love God's Word in a way I never had. I learned how to study the Bible from Professor Howard Hendricks. I learned what "systematic theology" was from S. Lewis Johnson, Stanley Toussaint, and others in the New Testament department. I learned how to share my faith in fresh ways from Haddon Robinson and what a Christian family looked like from Gene Getz.

One Thursday night during the second hour, Mrs. Witmer, the wife of the librarian, spoke to us about being ready to serve. I will never forget what she said. I listened carefully as she urged all of us as ministry-wives to be ready wherever God would take us. Whether our calling was to the mission field, the pastorate, or the Bible college or seminary, we should have some Scripture, some devotional on the back burner to encourage the women God may be calling us to serve. *"It's like having a pot of soup on the back burner at home. When anyone comes, you have something to give."*

The notion that I would mingle like that with women was not on my radar screen. I never imagined myself teaching women. School teaching and studying the Bible were my personal passions. It never occurred to me to speak publicly or lead a Bible study. But as God began to teach me through His Word, through the godly women with whom I came in contact, and through the urging of my husband, my perspective changed. Like Humpty Dumpty, I did not seek to jump; I was pushed! But unlike Humpty Dumpty, the King—in the power of His Holy Spirit—put people in my life who taught me the importance of nurturing and nourishing women in my life. He alone has put the broken pieces of my life together. I will never get over the fact that the awesome, sovereign, gracious God of the universe has asked for my cooperation in His eternal purposes. I am humbled, and I rejoice at the privilege of serving what He has first taught me.

Today, my passion is that the women of my generation and the one following will once again open up the ancient Scriptures and find it life-giving, thirst-quenching, and freeing beyond belief. My passion is that we would *receive and obey God's Word,* not only when we feel like it or if it makes sense, but immediately and joyfully as the Thessalonians did, so it will spread rapidly and not be dishonored. My passion for the women God so graciously has placed in my life, beginning with my two lovely daughters and one daughter-in-law, is that we would daily, consistently, faithfully, intentionally, and deliberately teach what is good (Titus 2:3–5).

My prayer for all women who call themselves Christ followers is that we would not be so quick to embrace the culture of our times. The voices shouting for our attention will someday die. The eternal principles of God remain. I pray that as women of this generation we will rediscover the high honor and dignity given to us by the Ancient of Days because we belong to His Son. I pray that we will learn how to celebrate our uniqueness as we function within the local church in harmony with men. I pray that every one of us will take a long, hard look at the local church in which God has put us and at the leadership God has given us and resolve to contribute to our church's spiritual health, not her demise. Only then will our local churches become the healthy places where true ministry happens, by women, for women, and through women.

THINK IT OVER

1. What are some areas of strength in the way your earthly family works together? Why are these characteristics important in your family?

2. Describe how your family shares responsibilities for the management of your home.

3. How would someone know that your church understands it is a family of believers?

4. Who in your church takes responsibility for the spiritual health of its members?

5. What do the leaders in your church envision a fully developed Christ follower to look like?

THINK IT THROUGH

The way to fill your mind with God's truth is to chew on a few verses so you can keep the focus God has on what He is doing in and through Christ followers today.

"They devoted themselves to the apostles' teaching and to the fellowship, to the breaking of bread and to prayer. . . . All the believers were together and had everything in common. . . . Every day they continued to meet together in the temple courts. They broke bread in their homes and ate together with glad and sincere hearts." (Acts 2:42, 44, 46)

"Consequently, you are no longer foreigners and aliens, but fellow citizens with God's people and members of God's household, built on the foundation of the apostles and prophets, with Christ Jesus himself as the chief cornerstone. In him the whole building is joined together and rises to become a holy temple in the Lord. And in him you too are being built together to become a dwelling in which God lives by his Spirit." (Ephesians 2:19–22)

"This mystery is that through the gospel the Gentiles are heirs together with Israel, members together of one body, and sharers together in the promise in Christ Jesus. . . . His intent was that now, through the church, the manifold wisdom of

God should be made known *to the rulers and authorities in the heavenly realms,* according to his eternal purpose which he accomplished in Christ Jesus our Lord." (Ephesians 3:6, 10–11, emphasis added)

"After all, no one ever hated his own body, but he feeds and cares for it, just as Christ does the church—for we are members of his body. . . . This is a profound mystery— but I am talking about Christ and the church." (Ephesians 5:29–30, 32)

"As you come to him, the living Stone—rejected by men but chosen by God and precious to him—you also, like living stones, are being built into a spiritual house to be a holy priesthood, offering spiritual sacrifices acceptable to God through Jesus Christ. . . . But you are a chosen people, a royal priesthood, a holy nation, a people belonging to God, that you may declare the praises of him who called you out of darkness into his wonderful light." (1 Peter 2:4–5, 9)

Chapter Three

THINGS IN COMMON

"Women in my generation need a church where the leaders value spiritual health over numerical growth, godliness over greatness and holy purposes over programs with the goal that the family of God can grow together."

RUTH VANGROUW, Women's Ministries Leader

"My father's life as we witnessed it was more eloquent than anything he ever said. As an adult I have become aware of his simplicity, humility and integrity, as well as of many other qualities of which a child would take no notice. . . . Like his Master he 'rose a great while before day.' He went downstairs in his robe . . . to kneel in prayer and study his Bible before breakfast. The difference it made to us to know that we had been thus prayed for every day before we were awake was unperceived then, and only God can assess the long-term effects of those prayers throughout the rest of our lives."

ELISABETH ELLIOT, *The Shaping of a Christian Family*, 55.

"The greatest thing the leaders in that little church did many years ago was teach my mother and father how to lead our family. What they did at home, they carried to church. They weren't perfect, but they were content to do their part in the grand scheme of God."

"Now the overseer must be above reproach, the husband of but one wife, temperate, self-controlled, respectable, hospitable, able to teach, not given to drunkenness, not violent but gentle, not quarrelsome, not a lover of money. He must manage his own family well and see that his children obey him with proper respect."

1 Timothy 3:2-4

Chapter Three

THINGS IN COMMON

The young boy stood waiting at the window for his packet. He drew his thin jacket around him, trying to fend off the wind. World War I had ended, and there was little money to care for a family of nine. The lad's father had gone to the New World to stake out a new life, ignorant of the needs of his children. Now, with no money for an education, the fourteen-year-old boy, fifth in the family, had to make a decision. He'd heard that his uncle, the ship captain, was in town. They were looking for strong young men. With few other choices, he signed up to be a sailor.

"Here's your packet, sonny."

The flat brown paper wrap concealed a pillow, a single blanket, some toiletries, and a day's rations—hardly enough for a hungry sailor after a long night's watch. The salt air filled his nostrils. The thought of leaving his homeland frightened him.

"Anchors aweigh!"

On board, he waved to no one; his mother had the little ones to care for. As the ship slipped away from the Cardiff dock, he remembered how some men from his town had gone to sea and never returned. Two secret longings filled the young man's heart as the ship entered the open seas. He hoped to meet up with his oldest brother, Danny, the youngest captain in the Merchant Marines, and he longed to see his father.

Four years at sea only magnified the man's distaste for his job. Overcome by the longing to see and know his father, he jumped ship in Baltimore, Maryland, and traveled through Chicago by train to Canada to find his father. He arrived in Manitoba with great hopes. When he found his father, he was devastated. His father was living with another woman and her child.

What the boy, my father, was looking for has been identified as "father hunger," a longing that infects the heart of a son for his father because of desertion or separation. In preindustrial societies, men and boys largely worked together. With the industrial revolution, things changed. Fathers and sons were together for only small amounts of time. Today, with the increasing acceptance of divorce and unwed pregnancy, the negative effects of "father hunger" are rampant. And they are not restricted to boys. Girls experience a negative effect as well, especially in adolescence. Both sons and daughters have a sense of loss when the father of the family is absent.

But God had another family for my father. On the way to see his father, my father traveled from Baltimore through Chicago to Duluth and up over the US/Canadian border. A man got on the train in Chicago and sat beside him all the way to Winnipeg. They discovered they had many things in common. Both were Welshmen. Both had come to live in the new world. Both were going to Winnipeg. The older Welshman, Mr. Evans, listened to the younger man's story and told him the old, old story of Jesus, inviting him to trust Him. My father did not believe at that time, but before they parted, Mr. Evans invited Leslie Jones home for Christmas dinner in case he couldn't find his father. Disappointed with his own father, my father took Mr. Evans up on his offer and went to his home. In the months that followed, Mr. Evans invited my father to attend services where he heard of the love of the heavenly Father who sent the Son to be his Savior. He trusted Christ on a cold Winnipeg night, sitting on a city tram thinking about Isaiah 53:6. It was the only Bible verse in English he knew, but he did what the preacher had said: Put your name in the spaces. That is when he found his eternal Father and accepted His Son as his Savior.

None of my father's brothers or sisters came to trust in the Lord Jesus Christ personally. I cannot explain to you the ways of God in this case. I can only tell you He is sovereign and has shown my father and mother (who was the oldest daughter of Mr. Evans!) great kindness. In our little family of four children, each knows the Savior. And each of our families has heard the gospel and trusted Christ. I do not understand the ways of God, but I love to see how He works and I know I can trust His heart.

FATHERS IN GOD'S FAMILY

The story of my father's conversion is an amazing one of God's sovereign grace. It is also a good reminder of the needs people have in common, which include the need for a good father in the home, the need for the family to have a leader who loves them. It is a good reminder of the pain many feel when a godly father is absent or he abandons the family unit.

In the church my father attended he met men who took him under their wings. It wasn't a perfect church. No such thing exists. But in that local church in Winnipeg, Manitoba, he met men who fathered him as a son. It had a few godly leaders. It had brothers and sisters, mothers and fathers who welcomed my father and helped him learn what it meant to serve God's purposes.

Coming to a community of believers makes all the difference for men and women as they grow into fully developed Christ followers. Within the safety of a healthy local church we learn the importance of biblical values. In the context of a local church we meet godly women who are willing to take young brides like my mother and teach her the importance of prayer, teaching her what is good and how to love her new husband and her children. Ultimately it is in the context of the local church where people like my mother and father learn to manage family and home (1 Timothy 3 and Titus 2:3–8) and practice a newfound faith in Christ.

HEALTHY CHURCHES HAVE CERTAIN THINGS IN COMMON

In the same way godly men bring strong leadership to the human family for its ultimate good, so men willing to be godly bring a spiritual strength to the local church that nothing on earth can replace. They provide the protection and leadership it needs as the natural spiritual nursery where babies are born and children are brought to maturity. When fathers take their responsibility of leadership in the family and the church, the negative effects of abandonment do not occur. As newborns and growing children of God, we are fathered and mothered by those who have walked the journey longer than we have. We are led by those who have learned to trust the ways of God. In that context we learn God's eternal purposes for our lives. The surprising truth is this: *We will never outgrow our need to be nourished* by the church. *We must always be closely connected* with a local group of God's people who value His Word for spiritual and interpersonal relational growth. We will always need godly leadership, even more as the day of Christ's return approaches (Hebrews 10:25).

Just as God's purpose for the family is born out of His creative wisdom, so His purpose for the local church is born out of His eternal plan. His purpose for the church is not a whim of culture. Nor is it without mystery. But, like the mystery of the unity in the Godhead and the uniqueness of each Member's role, so the church bears the stamp of ownership of the triune God. His purposes reflect a set of priorities that spiritually healthy churches will embrace so the family of God stays healthy. Without this spiritual health, the church cannot expect to give birth to spiritually healthy babies. Without embracing the God-given family roles for men and women in His church, her members won't take seriously the responsibilities assigned to each family member. (See "Epilogue: A Word to Church Leaders" for more information on this process.)

What is it that makes believing communities spiritually healthy? What characteristics do they share that show they understand God's purposes for His family? What values do they own for the spiritual good of their members and the glory of God?

Many books have been written in this generation on the importance of church health. Every author lists what he or she considers to be the essential marks of a healthy church. (See sample core values on pp. 184-86) My purpose is not to repeat what has been said elsewhere. But since we are focusing on the arena of the local church as the primary place where women should minister to women, it is fitting to identify the spiritual core values churches hold when they commit to growing both men and women to become fully developed Christ followers.

The five characteristics are not inspired, but they are reflected in the New Testament church and provide the spiritual atmosphere necessary for any local family of God—boys and girls, men and women—to grow to spiritual maturity.

Value One: Christ Alone Is the Head of the Church

A healthy church acknowledges that Christ alone is the Head of the church and that His Word to the church is our final answer. The church that functions as a family recognizes the need for the centrality of Scripture. Only God's Word used by the Holy Spirit will establish believers in the faith and make them strong in Christ. The healthy church values God's Christ as the ultimate model to follow and places God's Word at the center of its life. Few believed this more strongly than Peter, who personally acclaimed the Lord Jesus as God's Christ (Messiah). It was to Peter and the other disciples that Jesus said: "This was not revealed to you by man, but by my Father in heaven. . . . On this rock I will build my church, and the gates of Hades will not overcome it" (Matthew 16:17–18).

That means no program, no person, no organization can demand loyalty that competes with the final authority of Christ in His Word. No one competes for His glory. No one adds or subtracts from His commands. What

He has spoken to us, He intends for us to obey. There is no new plan for this century that has not already been given. In these last days, the Word we need to hear is spoken by the Son (Hebrews 1:1–2). We must obey Him.

Most of us agree with this first value. Yet all of us at some point find ourselves excusing certain attitudes and behaviors and ignoring other statements God has made, explaining them away because they don't fit or suit our culture. So if we understand what God is saying when He makes Christ the Head of the church and asks the family to obey Him, we need to be careful in accurately interpreting the Bible. Unless we are consistent in how we explain what Christ asks us to obey, we will misuse the ancient text and ignore the importance of obeying it today.

It has been helpful to me to think of four basic truths that help me understand how to understand *what God meant by what He said*. They determine how I listen to and obey God's Word.

God Has Revealed Himself to Us. He has spoken in creation to show us His power and divine nature (Romans 1:20). He has told us what we need to know in order to live life in a godly manner (2 Peter 1:3). In the past, He told the fathers what He wanted them to know through the prophets (Hebrews 1:1–2), but in these last days, we see His glory, the revelation of Himself in His Son (John 1:14). If you had no other book than the Bible (many of our brothers and sisters around the world don't), you would have everything you need to please God. He has revealed Himself to us, and the healthy church acknowledges the Headship of Christ in the church and knows God's revelation.

God Has Spoken the Truth. From Genesis to Revelation, the record of inspired Scripture is that God does not lie (Numbers 23:19; Titus 1:2), that Jesus Christ, the God-man, *is* the truth and the way to truth (John 14:6). That means when I open God's Word, I am to recognize its historical and theological truthfulness as well as its literary qualities. Because its source is God the Holy Spirit, I must recognize its *supernatural nature.* It is a book from God about the one true God (1 Thessalonians 2:13). Listen to what Paul says about it to the pastor Timothy, as Timothy faces false teachers who threaten to destroy the local church in Ephesus:

> *But as for you, continue in what you have learned and have become convinced of, because you know those from whom you learned it, and how from infancy you have known the holy Scriptures, which are able to make you wise for salvation through faith in Christ*

Jesus. All Scripture is God-breathed and is useful for teaching, rebuking, correcting and training in righteousness, so that the man of God may be thoroughly equipped for every good work. (2 Timothy 3:14–17)

God's truth makes me wise and is useful for the most important things in my life. I am not to argue with Scripture's contents because it bears the very signature of God. In Scripture, He has spoken the truth. To add to His truth or subtract from His truth or ignore His truth is to act to the detriment of my life and the local church to which I belong.

God Weaves His Truth Through Story. God has not spoken to us by way of a blimp in the sky or through a dictionary or an encyclopedia. He has not alphabetized His words or presented His thoughts in a systematized way. God has placed His truth in a context we understand: the context of man's story and the context of time and space. God begins with "In the beginning . . ." (Genesis 1:1) and He ends with ". . . a new heaven and a new earth . . . " (Revelation 21:1). Every story in between of men and women carries the truths that God has set down. Like spiritual gravity in the universe, God's truth holds the stories together. And they are stories of real people, of real families, of real problems, and of God's real enabling power to make the difference.

Therefore, when I want to know what a godly leader looks like, I listen to what God values as I read real-life stories in His Word. I listen to what God expects from their lives. I look intently as their personal stories unfold and listen for what God praises. When I want to know what God expects me as a woman to obey, I read the commands addressed to women in the context of towns, families, workplaces, and the local church. I listen for what He praises so I too can please Him. Paul's letters to Timothy prove this fact as he comes to the end of his own life's story. He leaves Timothy with important instructions on how to behave and what to do in the context of the church: "Although I hope to come to you soon, I am writing you these instructions so that, if I am delayed, you will know how people ought to conduct themselves in God's household, which is the church of the living God, the pillar and foundation of the truth" (1 Timothy 3:14–15).

Healthy churches, then, pay attention to the story of the church in the New Testament. They read the letters written by the apostles and understand how the truth God revealed should be obeyed in our time.

God's Truth Is Given Birth Through Symbols. The essence of metaphor and simile is understanding and experiencing one kind of thing in terms of another. It is the bringing together of two different things so that we understand the truth borne by the connection. Peter uses simile when he calls believers to grow up. "Like newborn babies, crave pure spiritual milk, so that by it you may grow up in your salvation, now that you have tasted that the Lord is good" (1 Peter 2:2–3). Anyone who has heard a hungry baby cry or watched a child latch on to the mother's breast has no doubt in her mind the attitude Peter says Christ followers should have as they hunger for God's truth. If there is no craving, there is no health. The problem is not with the milk; the problem is with the lack of hunger!

There are many places in Scripture where God's truth is borne out through imagery. The expectation is that we will make the connection. When we do, we will understand how when the two different things are brought together, we will know what kind of people to be.

Value Two: Godly Leaders Take Responsibility to Teach God's Word

A second quality of a healthy church is one in which godly leaders take responsibility to teach God's Word and lead with authority. Healthy churches understand the need for godly leadership and authority. When there is a vacuum of leadership, the family knows the feelings of abandonment.

Even a cursory look at the writings of the New Testament identifies the fact that godly leaders were a key to health in the early church. In Acts, the leaders at Pentecost were men whom Jesus personally taught. Formerly timid Peter preached a sermon of power (see Acts 2:14–41). When a problem of need arose in the early church (the Grecian Jewish widows were being overlooked), the Twelve (Matthias having replaced Judas in Acts 1:12–26) gave godly leadership and said, "It would not be right for us to neglect the ministry of the word of God in order to wait on tables. Brothers, choose seven men from among you who are known to be full of the Spirit and wisdom. We will turn this responsibility over to them and will give our attention to prayer and the ministry of the word" (Acts 6:2–4). It is from these seven that later stipulations are given concerning serving done by deacons in the church (1 Timothy 3:8–16).

The council of Jerusalem bears witness to a watershed decision of godly leadership in the early church. The team of James, the half brother of the Lord and spokesman for the rest, Peter, Paul, and Barnabas brings the issue to the apostles, elders, and the whole church of whether or not to ask Gentile believers to take on the Jewish tradition of circumcision. The letter telling the decision not to require it is signed by those in authority in the church: the apostles and the elders (Acts 15:6–29).

Godly Leaders Shepherd the Flock. The New Testament uses two kinds of words to describe how leadership is recognized in the local church. The first was "flock" words, as in Acts 20:28 where Paul says, "Keep watch over yourselves and all the flock of which the Holy Spirit has made you overseers." Peter picks up similar words in 1 Peter 5:1–3 when he says:

> *To the elders among you, I appeal as a fellow elder: . . . Be shepherds of God's flock that is under your care, serving as overseers—not because you must, but because you are willing, as God wants you to be; not greedy for money, but eager to serve; not lording it over those entrusted to you, but being examples to the flock.*

This request was not unusual to Peter. The Great Shepherd Himself had taught him in a conversation Peter would never forget!

"Do you truly love me? . . . Feed my lambs."

"Do you truly love me? . . . Take care of my sheep."

"Do you love me? . . . Feed my sheep" (John 21:15–23).

We stayed for a few days on a sheep farm in the Southern Hemisphere. I have seen what shepherds do in Australia and New Zealand. *They lead the flock* to green pasture. *They take seriously the care* of the sheep as they graze on the land. They lead them to water and often offer them a salt block to lick for enjoyment. *They watch out for them and protect them from predators.* If the sheep fall over, the shepherd *turns them back onto their feet.* No sheep has the ability on its own to set itself back onto its feet. The sheep are entirely dependent on the shepherd.

I have also watched Robin, the shepherd's wife, help the shepherd with a sick lamb, a ewe's broken limb, or a sheep's torn flesh. The picture that stands out in my mind is one in which she bathed the sheep with water where the fox had bitten his leg and poured on oil to heal it. Her partnership with the shepherd made it possible for the sheep to get well.

Healthy churches appoint leaders who shepherd the flock well. They don't do it for power, prestige, or a lot of money. They just know the Scripture expects the leadership in a local church to behave like shepherds with a flock. When they do, the elders as a group pastor or shepherd the flock for its own good.

Godly Leaders Oversee the Church. The other kind of word used to address the leadership in the local church is a family word that Paul uses in what are known as his pastoral letters. Paul instructs Pastor Timothy to make sure that the men he appoints as elders are qualified to "oversee" (rule) in the church because of the way they manage their family at home. The qualifications given in 1 Timothy 3:1–7 identify clearly the kind of leaders Paul expects Timothy to look for:

Here is a trustworthy saying: If anyone sets his heart on being an overseer, he desires a noble task. Now the overseer must be above reproach, the husband of but one wife, temperate, self-controlled, respectable, hospitable, able to teach, not given to drunkenness, not violent but gentle, not quarrelsome, not a lover of money. He must manage his own family well and see that his children obey him with proper respect. (If anyone does not know how to manage his own family, how can he take care of God's church?) He must not be a recent convert, or he may become conceited and fall under the same judgment as the devil. He must also have a good reputation with outsiders, so that he will not fall into disgrace and into the devil's trap.

What a list. You may be looking at your church leaders and asking, "Can any man ever live up to these qualifications?" Not without being dependent on the Spirit of God to transform him into a godly leader. Acts 6:35 records the basis on which leaders were chosen: "Brothers, choose seven men from among you *who are known to be full of the Spirit and wisdom* ... They chose Stephen, a man full of faith and of the Holy Spirit;" (italics added). Whether you have leaders like that or not, pray that God will make the leadership in your church healthy. If your leaders are not healthy, your church will never be!

Value Three: Members Are Equally Loved and Valued

A third marker of a healthy church is one where every member is known to be well loved and considered equal in value, taking seriously the responsibilities within his or her sphere. But perhaps as you have read the Scriptures quoted, you see a "family" order showing up. The truth about a mother and father in a family is that although their equality in value is not disputed, their roles are not interchangeable. From the earliest chapters in Genesis, we learn that Eve shares Adam's physical nature (Genesis 2:21–23), and together they share God's image, God-given responsibilities, and dominion (Genesis 1:27–30). Eve stands alongside Adam as his helper and complement. They are bound together in a God-given unity and equality. But never is there a expectation of exchangeability or uniformity of responsibility. C. F. Hogg has said it well:

> *In Scripture there is nowhere any suggestion of the inferiority of the woman nor of the superiority of the man. Each is necessary to the other; they are complementary, not competitive; she was created to be a help meet for him, supplying what is lacking that together they might be complete (Genesis 5:2). That God is the Head of Christ does not make Christ inferior to God. That man is the head of the woman does not make her inferior to him. The man was "first formed," but they were created together, she having been "taken out of man," as it is written, "Male and female created He them" (Genesis 1:27).*[1]

Paul concurs with the mutual value when he says in Galatians 3:26–29:

> *You are all sons of God through faith in Christ Jesus, for all of you who were baptized into Christ have clothed yourselves with Christ. There is neither Jew nor Greek, slave nor free, male nor female, for you are all one in Christ Jesus. If you belong to Christ, then you are Abraham's seed, and heirs according to the promise.*

Healthy churches recognize that all members are equal in value before the cross. All must come through faith to Christ; none are excluded because of station in life, gender, or national history (see John 1:11–12). All are equal in value but different in God-given roles. Gloriously that means family members are not clones of each other; each has a distinct role and different gifts that do not deny others' value.

Value Four: A Healthy Church Recognizes and Embraces Diversity in Roles and Gifts

A fourth value is one to be discussed in length at the end of the book. It is enough to comment briefly on it at this point. Many years ago, my sixth-grade teacher called me "effervescent" on a report card. I thought it was a criticism, and I determined for the next six years that I would try to be non-emotional about the way I responded to things. When I finally realized that was not who I was, I began to enjoy being spontaneous again, getting excited about things like beautiful sunsets, lovely fabrics, soft fragrances, wonderful presents. Of course, that brought with it the reverse emotions: tears, grief, and other such feelings! As a young bride, I desperately wanted

Gary to respond as I did to any exciting news, answered prayers, and Christmas presents. But as you might imagine, we are married to each other because we like each other's differences. After a few years of marriage and children, I became so thankful that he *didn't* respond in the same ways I did. Oh, he felt deeply about some things, but the only time I heard him give shouts of joy was when his favorite football team won the game!

In the family of God, unity rather than uniformity is the goal. Diversity is the synergy that makes the family function well. Variety makes the body work. None of us are the same. No two of us have the same mix of natural talents, spiritual gifts, leadership style, or personality. The blending of differences in the local church family makes for harmony and mutual sensitivity. Paul makes this point in a grand way in his discussion of spiritual gifts in 1 Corinthians 12:14–15, 17–18, where he says:

> *Now the body is not made up of one part but of many. If the foot should say, "Because I am not a hand, I do not belong to the body," it would not for that reason cease to be part of the body. . . . If the whole body were an eye, where would the sense of hearing be? If the whole body were an ear, where would the sense of smell be? But in fact God has arranged the parts in the body, every one of them, just as he wanted them to be.*

It is not being the same that makes the body of believers function well together. It is valuing the other's difference. Men are not women. Women are not men. And all of us fit into the body as God has ordained. The healthy church takes differences very seriously so it allows harmony to be played in the orchestra of God's family.

Value Five: Family Members Mature and Share the Workload

A final value is the focus we have tried to set from the beginning of this book: maturity. If everyone in your church was like you in terms of your maturity quotient, how healthy would your church be? It is clear as you look at the Scriptures that the writers of the letters to the churches—James, Paul, Peter, John, and the writer of Hebrews—valued maturity. Maturity in James's terms is *persevering under trial* (James 1:12). James says immaturity is doubting God, not recognizing your need to ask Him for wisdom. Scripture describes maturity as being *"complete, not lacking anything"* (James 1:4) and being *"filled to the measure of all the fullness of God"* (Ephesians 3:19). In his first letter to the Corinthians, a gifted and energetic church, Paul warns that church's believers about their major problem: arrested spiritual development.

He says in 1 Corinthians 3:1–3 that he couldn't address them as spiritual because they were mere infants in Christ and he had to give them milk. He is not saying milk is unnecessary. Peter in 1 Peter 2:1–2 says that hunger for the milk of the Word is the proof a person is a believer. In fact, if you don't hunger for it, you may not know Christ at all! But Paul says that although a diet of milk, staying informed only of the elementary truths of the gospel, is essential, maturing believers go beyond spiritual babyhood. The writer in Hebrews helps us understand the idea when he says:

> We have much to say about this [about the superiority of the priesthood of Jesus Christ to the old system], but it is hard to explain because you are slow to learn. In fact, though by this time you ought to be teachers, you need someone to teach you the elementary truths of God's word all over again. You need milk, not solid food! Anyone who lives on milk, being still an infant, is not acquainted with the teaching about righteousness. But solid food is for the mature, who by constant use have trained themselves to distinguish good from evil. (Hebrews 5:11–14)

Paul's greatest insult to Christ followers who refuse to grow up is found in the term "mere men" (1 Corinthians 3:1–14). The Corinthians are jealous and quarreling and insist on behaving like infants. His solution to immaturity is found in 1 Corinthians 13:11 where love is described as the test of adulthood in Christian living. To place another person's good above your own is the ultimate standard of maturity and clearly reflects the heart of the Lord Jesus Christ. To "grow up" and become responsible to share the load of serving in the Christian family is the sign of maturity.

Peter says that primary signs of spiritual immaturity are arguing with and slandering (gossiping about) other believers and a lack of hunger for God's Word (1 Peter 2:1–2). Peter uses the word *holy* as the basis on which to describe maturity to his readers (1:16). He quotes from Moses' words in Leviticus 11:44–45 when he commands us to "Be holy, because I [He, the Lord] am holy." Peter teaches us that transformation and maturity keep Christ followers from being ineffective and unproductive (2 Peter 1:8).

John says that the truly grown-up child is the one who walks in the light (1 John 1:5–7), repents of sin, and loves God's children. John goes on to say that the mature child of God experiences continual transformation (1 John 5:1–5).

There is no doubt in the minds of the New Testament writers, who themselves watched how the Lord Jesus lived, as to the kind of people a healthy church plans to grow. This is not about how the church should be

organized. This is not even about careful strategies and marketing tech-
niques, leadership seminars, or conference attendees. It is a serious discussion that requires every family member to look deeply within the shadows
of his or her heart and ask: "Am I still an infant? What in my life proves I
am finally growing up and sharing the workload allotted to me in this
church? Do I use my gift in the context of this local church? Am I helping the local church of which I am a part to become what God intends it
to be because I am a fully developing, maturing Christ follower?"

No one person, no one group, can do the work alone. All Christ followers are asked to share the load. The church family will become healthy
only when fathers model leadership and mothers take responsibility.

A FINAL APPEAL

Something has happened in the last fifty years that has weakened the
multiplication of godly women in the local church. Because the church was
not focused on growing godly women within her walls, new resources developed outside the church. Women began to grow and minister to women.
As their personal growth increased, women ministering to women dimin-
ished within the church. Older women with spiritual gifts went missing.
The church suffered and younger women suffered.

There is a need to make a change. My appeal is this: Instead of women
clustering *outside the church,* why not commit to reconsider the purposes
of God for His church? In the spirit of Titus 2:3–5, why not focus on the
task of growing godly women *within the local church?* It is within the church
that the mingling of generations takes place. It is within the church that
the structure of pastors and elders allows the whole Christian family to learn
to respect and love each other.

When church leaders know Jesus Christ personally and take seriously
the sinful state of mankind, they understand that nurturing a generation toward godly living takes spiritual commitment. They recognize that it requires a *host of godly women* who care more about developing their character
than their bodies, who love God more than they love their own comfort, and
whose boast is not in the power or freedom they have seized but in the One
who is their Master. Spiritually healthy churches embrace their responsibility to enable women to fulfill their roles as partners with men in shep-
herding the generations under them. The church where women are freed
and encouraged to minister to women is a church prepared for spiritual
health. It is a church whose spiritual resources are healthy, whose spiritual

diet is nutritious, and whose spiritual priorities deliberately and intentionally follow the biblical design for the believing community. *The healthy church trains the whole family to become fully developed followers of Jesus Christ. That is how it releases its spiritual potential.*

This is all to say that women need a church where the regenerating work of the Holy Spirit is recognized, where the spiritual family structure is taken seriously, where God's Word is valued, and where plans are prayerfully made for Scripture to be taught and spiritual growth to occur. That church will have a womb ready for new spiritual babies. It will be a place with the resources necessary to grow the spiritual child into a maturing adult.

THINK IT OVER

All maturing Christ followers in a local church, men and women and youth, do their part. Take the following passages and identify who is responsible and what commands they are responsible for in order to see personal maturity and the spiritual health of your church.

1. The Great Calling—John 10:3–5; 21:18–19

   Who?_____

   What?_____

2. The Great Commission—Matthew 28:16–20

   Who?_____

   What?_____

3. The Great Commandment—John 15:9–17 (see also 1 John 4:11–12, 19–21)

   Who?_____

   What?_____

4. The Great Charge—Acts 1:4–8; 2:37–47 (see especially verse 42)

   Who?_____

   What?_____

5. The Great Challenge—Titus 2:1–5

   Who?_____

   What?_____

THINK IT THROUGH

The words of the Lord Jesus in the Gospels are instructions on which the New Testament church rests. The words of the New Testament Epistles are the way the infant and growing church followed the apostles' teaching. Read and meditate on Paul's instructions to Timothy in 1 Timothy 3:14–16. Verse 16 is wonderful to memorize in order to keep your focus for the church clear.

> [14] *Although I hope to come to you soon, I am writing you these instructions so that,* [15] *if I am delayed, you will know how people ought to conduct themselves in God's household, which is the church of the living God, the pillar and foundation of the truth.* [16] *Beyond all question, the mystery of godliness is great: He appeared in a body, was vindicated by the Spirit, was seen by angels, was preached among the nations, was believed on in the world, was taken up in glory.*

NOTE

1. C. F. Hogg, W. E. Vine, and W. R. Lewis, *The Ministy of Women* (London: Pickering and Inglis, 1936), 6.

WHAT KIND OF WOMAN DOES THE CHURCH NEED?

"My grandmother loved me. She taught me that outward appearances are not as important as inward attitudes. She taught me that God is my refuge. She lived frugally and served the poor by teaching them English using the Bible as her text. She was my confidante and a very good woman."

"The woman who has influenced me most in the church taught me to focus on Christ's esteem, that being a Christian is a spiritual life not a religion, that perseverance is a valuable quality in a woman, and that you can tell if a woman is wise by her words and her actions."

"My sister, Cindy, modeled a strong Christian character who loved Jesus with all her heart. She introduced me to Jesus Christ."

"She was my 'spiritual mom.' She loved me and lived what she taught. She knew God personally as well as intellectually; she was Christ to me."

BETH LAMPRECHT

"She loved God deeply, loved others well, and modeled faithfulness to the service she did in the church family. She never bailed on her commitments."

"Whoever can be trusted with very little can also be trusted with much, and whoever is dishonest with very little will also be dishonest with much. So if you have not been trustworthy in handling worldly wealth, who will trust you with true riches? And if you have not been trustworthy with someone else's property, who will give you property of your own?"

Luke 16:10–12

Chapter Four

WHAT KIND OF WOMAN DOES THE CHURCH NEED?

She was ninety-three with a steady gait.

Every month she arrived at my doorstep to clean the family silver. Each piece had been a wedding gift. Without her careful touch, the pieces sat unusable behind the glass hutch. With three children and a busy pastor-husband, cleaning silver wasn't at the top of my to-do list. I don't know how she knew about the need. She just called one day after our third child was born.

"This is Jean Oliver. I've been thinking about what I can do to help you. I'm too old to baby-sit the children. I can't lead the Bible study at the chapel or clean your house. Will you let me come and clean your silver? If it's anything like mine, it needs it all the time!"

"Thank you, Mrs. Oliver. I would love that!"

How did she know cleaning silver was not even on the list for any day in the near future? I never found out who told her my silver needed cleaning, and it didn't much matter. The phone call signaled the start of a long and close friendship between a lady sixty years my senior and me. She'd come at the stroke of 10 A.M. and leave by noon.

"I don't expect you to feed me lunch. Just let me do some things you can't do for yourself."

She did that and much more. Sometimes she talked about her youth, the changes that had taken place over the past century, how she'd had to adjust to things like telephones, cars, plastic wrap, throwaway dishes, television, and airplanes. Often she spoke thankfully about her family, the Elliots of Portland, the godliness of their lives. Repeatedly she shared spiritual wisdom with me on questions I asked about life, the church, and my family. And always, this spunky lady whose life traversed almost one hundred years promised to pray for me in things that overwhelmed me.

She modeled grace and godly poise. And best of all, my church held women like her in high honor. The members valued women who modeled a long obedience to Christ in the same direction. Women who didn't need someone to convince them to minister to other women. Women who ministered to other women because God's Word said they should.

I cried when Mrs. Oliver died, but not because my silver tray and teapot sat tarnished. I cried because I'd lost a precious treasure. This woman, so full of life long into her nineties, saw needs in my life that went deeper than the surface of a tray. She did what gracious, godly women do. She helped me manage life. She chose to invest small moments of time that today yield daily returns in my life. Before Mrs. Oliver left for heaven, her daughter, well schooled in love for God and deeds of kindness, became a mentor in my life.

With no program to follow or committee in our church to tell her what she should do, Mrs. Oliver modeled a godly heart and the fruit of her life overflowed into mine. The leaders in our church respected women like her. They recognized the importance of women ministering in practical ways and in spiritual ways to other women.

Looking back, I see a host of women in my life who have walked with God for a lifetime. Most did what they did because they believed that preparing a new generation of women to live for God was the most important thing they could do in their church. Many came into my life by serendipitous means. All were under a conviction that influencing women toward godliness is central to church health. When the church values the development of godly women and godly women take their responsibility seriously, the potential for the spiritual health of the church is enormous.

It is appropriate then to ask, "What kind of woman do our churches need for ministry to occur between women in the local church?" I am frequently asked questions like that. A young woman enrolled in seminary walks into my office and asks, "What kind of qualifications does a woman need to lead in women's ministries in the church?" Most often a church member who is eager to serve wants to know, "How can I be the woman God needs in order to serve women?"

My answer invariably contains several ideas. Let's look at them.

THE CHURCH NEEDS WOMEN WHO LOVE WOMEN

First, the church needs *women who love women and are convinced there is eternal value in working with them*. The stories in Scripture confirm that God's women have behaved like this for centuries. The Bible shows the powerful influence godly women have in the scheme of things. They model holy traits and cause permanent changes in their world. They are women who are willing to spend time being *with* women. That is the first thing. It is what your church needs. It is why the leaders in church should look for women in the local church who care for younger women, who serve needs beyond themselves. These women spend meaningful time together.

Not every woman who calls herself a Christ follower likes women. That does not change the need or the mandate that the church needs women who love women. The time in which we live maximizes this need for women to serve women. Because of this, I regularly caution women who work in women's ministries with me: "If you don't *like* these women, they will know it!" If you don't love them, don't work with them. Animosity is a hard thing to hide.

The Church Needs Women Who Love God's Word

Second, the church needs *women who love God's truth and recognize there is a biblical mandate for women to work with women.* For years people have discussed what women and men should be doing in the local church and what roles each should have. What responsibilities should each take? Others have drafted well-documented treatises on such topics, some books of which are included in the bibliography at the end of this book. But no man or woman reading God's Word can escape the mandate that it holds for women to teach women.

It is a mandate relevant for the church in the twenty-first century, yet it is often minimized or ignored. It comes with no cultural limitations. It simply states how things should function in the family of local believers. It reminds us that the need of the moment in a post-Christian world is to return to God's statements of truth. It reminds us that the experience of programs will never produce Christ followers who are learning to handle the Word of God. The church has tried programs only to come to the discovery that ignorance of God's Word abounds.

Observing the need only makes the Titus 2 mandate more relevant than ever. The church needs women who love God's truth and are able to teach what is good. The church needs women who model godly disciplines so they may qualify to teach what is good.

Several things are clear from Titus 2:3–5. *Godly women are among the greatest resources in the church,* as are godly men. The spiritually healthy church will intentionally prioritize developing godly women. As shepherds or pastors teach sound doctrine in the context of their churches, they prepare godly women to invest in other women's lives. The motivation Paul states is amazing: No one will malign the Word of God.

Many godly women have shaped my life. In turn, I have had the privilege of influencing others. In both cases, women who lead with godly poise in the local church take seriously the traits Paul says will cultivate spiritual health in women. I call them "SMARTS."

THE CHURCH NEEDS WOMEN WITH SMARTS

It is obvious to anyone who builds that the quality of a building is determined by the quality of the materials used. In a silly way, the story of the Three Little Pigs teaches us that. The wolf could never blow down the house built of bricks. The houses built with straw or sticks had no ability to stand.

When the Lord Jesus Christ told Peter and the other disciples in Matthew 16:13–20 that He would build His church, He did not explain that He was talking about men-and-women materials. Standing in Caesarea Philippi, twenty-five miles north of Jerusalem beneath the rugged rock hovering over them, the disciples may have thought His plans included other substances. They would know the limestone, gold, and precious stones of the temple that gleamed in the Jerusalem sun. But His promise that day was "The gates of Hades will not overcome it." Whatever the building blocks, they would defy death. *How* He would do this incredible thing remained a mystery until after Pentecost. They were only asked to wait in Jerusalem until the Holy Spirit came on them in power. When the Holy Spirit came, He came in life-changing power so that every man and woman baptized into the body of Christ becomes a spiritual living stone. The preferred plan for the Lord Jesus as He builds His church is no different today than it was then. What do we need to do to join Him? We need women with "SMARTS" (an acronym for six primary attributes the godly woman possesses).

The Church Needs Women Who Are SPIRITUAL

First, the church needs women who are *spiritual*. In a time when it is popular to be spiritual, it is important to state what the Bible defines as spiritual. In order to appreciate what Christian spirituality is, we must first clarify what it is not. Biblical spirituality is not channeling or mystical asceticism that shows contempt for the material world. It is not Eastern thought that lifts up human wisdom as a god. Nor is it focused on human reasoning, as in Greek thought. These are not true connections to biblical spirituality. In *Restoring the Soul,* Miriam Bundy helps us understand the fallacy of present-day attempts to be spiritual. She says: "Throughout the ages, many diametrically opposed belief systems have issued a claim on spirituality. From New Age to the occult, from scientism to supernaturalism, from Buddhism to naturalism, proponents of these creeds profess to be spiritual. . . . The search for [this kind of] spirituality may be gaining popularity, but it is not new."[1] Then she points out that Isaiah confirms this when he asks: "When men tell you to consult mediums and spiritists, who whisper and mutter, should not a people inquire of their God? Why consult the dead on behalf of the living?" (Isaiah 8:19).

True Christian spirituality begins when the Lord Jesus Christ redeems us from our sin and eternal death at the moment of new birth (see John 3:8 and 16). The word *spiritual* describes the supernatural relationship a human being enjoys with God through the personal power of the Holy Spirit. This "being made alive" by the Holy Spirit is the only basis on which the human being can live with hope (Galatians 5:16–25). The only absolute and trustworthy standard for spirituality is found in God's Word. The only Source of true spirituality is the Holy Spirit, the third person of the Trinity. Spirituality then is not a self-help program but a process of knowing God and of becoming holy.

The woman who influences other women for good and God's glory is concerned first about her spiritual relationship to the one true God. She cares to know the God who came to earth in human flesh, died on a cross, and rose the third day from death. To be spiritual in the Christian sense is to be exclusive about your devotion and passionate about things like sin, repentance, forgiveness, and discipleship. Christian spirituality is Christo-centric because of the union one enjoys with Jesus Christ.

Some questions that help distinguish whether a woman is spiritual can be used as a personal checklist for yourself and others you serve alongside.

1. Have I been born of the Spirit? Do I know I have eternal life? (2 Corinthians 5:17)
2. Do I have a heart to know the one true God, the God of the Bible? (John 20:30–31)
3. Do I hunger to know God's Word? Do I know and practice it? (1 Peter 2:1–7)
4. Do I care to get to know God better through meditation and prayer? (1 Thessalonians 5:17)

5. Do I see myself changing to look like Jesus as I practice godly disciplines? (1 Thessalonians 1:7)

The truth of it is that spiritual women spend personal time with the Lord Jesus. They actively cultivate their spiritual lives. If you follow them around their house or office, you find them seeking to live in the presence of God. The church *needs* women who are *spiritual*.

The Church Needs Women Who Are MATURE

A second need exists in terms of the kind of woman the church needs: women who are *mature*. Paul uses the idea of maturity as the purpose statement for his life in relationship to what he does. "We proclaim him, admonishing and teaching everyone with all wisdom, so that we may present everyone perfect in Christ. To this end I labor, struggling with all his energy, which so powerfully works in me" (Colossians 1:28–29).

The writer of Hebrews in 6:1 urges his readers to "go on to maturity."

In secular Greek, the word *teleios* (mature, perfect, complete) means an adult, full-grown, as opposed to immature and infantile.

Going back to the metaphor of the family unit, you can easily see comparisons between maturity and immaturity. Babies are fun to have around, but they are messy, are self-centered, and know nothing about serving others. Babies and children need to be taught skills for living that will allow them to someday live as mature adults. All of us have been babies and youngsters at one time, but it is hard to imagine what our families would be like if none of us ever grew up!

The church needs women who are grown up. Mature women are skilled in the art of relationships. They are grown up in the way they handle life and a variety of circumstances. When a woman is mature, she is other-centered and has the heart of a servant. She can deal with all kinds of women in all stages and ages. She cares more about developing people than programs. She knows one cannot package the process of "wholeness" that describes how a person begins to look more and more like the Lord Jesus. A mature woman handles conflict with calmness and primarily is a grace-giver in the way she responds to women. The spiritually mature woman is a gift to her church, and the church needs women who minister to women to be mature. She seeks not to control but to serve.

The Church Needs Women Who Are ABLE

Related to being spiritually mature is the area of "being able." It includes being available but emphasizes the latter part of the word. The local church needs women who are *able*.

When I began to teach Leadership Development Workshops around the country, a lady called my office. She said: "Could you please change the words you are using? Some of us who want to come to the seminar are offended by the term *leadership*. We aren't all leaders! We aren't all able to lead!"

In an attempt to help women understand the impact they can have on others, I changed the terminology of the individual workshops but kept the meaning. If you think of leadership as being something you do way out in front of people, you may not be thinking of it correctly. But if you think of it as the ability to influence someone for good because of God's natural and spiritual gifts to you, then you are able to lead because you are making a difference in another woman's life. Spiritual leadership is *being able to influence others* for good and God's glory.

Sometimes it is difficult for a woman to admit she's a leader. But the church benefits when a godly woman who is competent and confident in her area of leadership (influence) equips women to live with skill.

Being able is about knowing the gifts God has personally given to you. *Being able* is about knowing what to do with those resources and when to use them. But it is more. Able women are team builders. They know the gifts God has given others and are more concerned with building a functioning team than with building their personal ministry. They are able to articulate a vision, strategize to achieve it, and inspire others to embrace it.

A woman who models this in the Old Testament is Abigail. Married to a surly and mean man called Nabal, she did for David, the anointed king, what her husband would not do. Though David and his men had protected Nabal's flocks and possessions, Nabal refused to honor them for their work. To save her household from disaster, Abigail "lost no time" and used her intelligence, her resources, and her ability to bring her servants together and serve David's needs (1 Samuel 25). The church needs women who are able.

The Church Needs Women Who Are RESPONSIBLE

The church of Jesus Christ in this century needs *responsible* women. Churches often dispute who is responsible for what. The woman who is a responsible Christ follower knows three things.

- She knows the truths of Scripture.
- She knows the real needs and the felt needs of the women around her.
- She knows how to creatively bridge the gap between the two.

Titus 2:3–4 calls it "teaching" and "training." Godly women are responsible to take the initiative in teaching, admonishing, discipling, and exhorting younger women in things about which men know very little and about which they should not be teaching.

The *American Heritage Dictionary* defines *responsible* as "liable to be required to give account, as of one's actions." Being responsible means I know what is asked of me based on Scripture in the context of the local church, my family, and the culture in which I live.

The aged Elizabeth, full of child as she meets Mary the pregnant virgin at her front door, acts responsibly toward the mother of our Lord. For three months she probably taught Mary everything she knew about this mysterious state of pregnancy. For three months they spoke together about the Holy One of Israel whose name they honored and whose will they trusted (Luke 1:39–45). Elizabeth's choice to be *responsible* to Mary was an extension of her character, as Luke emphasizes. "Both of them [Elizabeth and Zechariah] were upright in the sight of God, observing all the Lord's commandments and regulations blamelessly. But they had no children, because Elizabeth was barren" (Luke 1:6–7).

The woman Lydia, a dealer in purple cloth whose heart God opened, opens her home to the newly birthed church in Philippi (Acts 16:13–15). You can be sure she would have asked the women with whom she prayed at the water's edge, had they come to faith, to come home after her baptism. No one can forget Dorcas of Joppa who Luke says "was always doing good and helping the poor" (Acts 9:36). The weeping widows who stood around her dead body and showed Peter the robes and clothing Dorcas had sewn are a testimony to a responsible woman of God (see Acts 9:36–42). And Priscilla, a Jewish woman living in Corinth, shows responsibility as a Christian businesswoman as well as a theologian. She made tents to pay her bills and, with her husband Aquila, taught God's ways more accurately to Apollos (see Acts 18:24–28). The church of this century still needs women who respond to the physical and spiritual needs of the moment. When women are responsible in meeting the need of the moment, they are what the church of Jesus Christ needs.

Spiritual, mature, able, and responsible women also share another characteristic.

The Church Needs Women Who Are TEACHABLE

Betty is humble. In her senior years now, she has served the Lord as the wife of a Mission Aviation Fellowship pilot for fifty years. As fully developed Christ followers, Betty and her husband are in the family for the long haul. They just celebrated their fiftieth wedding anniversary, putting them in a category that is rare these days.

Yet every Wednesday for many years, Betty has joined in the women's Bible study. For many of those years, she was a small group leader. This year she has become a mentor for young mothers. When I asked the women to write what they hoped to learn this year in Bible study, Betty wrote this: "For many years I have taken the role of teacher, helping women to learn God's Word. This year, I am not a leader but I think God wants me to begin learning once again to be a learner. Some of that will be learning from my small group leader. Some of it will come from the young mothers as I mentor them in godly ways."

Betty supports the leader, who is the age of her daughter, and Betty is *teachable*. A teachable spirit is invaluable when it comes to making a difference in women's lives. It is irreplaceable when women work with men and women in the context of the local church.

Remember the mandate Paul gave to women in Titus 2:3–5? He *assumes* that women in Crete will listen to Titus's sound doctrine (Titus 2:1) as he teaches them to teach younger women. He expects them to be there in the meeting of the church while the apostles' teaching is taught (see Acts 2:42). As they listen, their teachable spirit is evident in how they relate to their leaders, their pastor, the older men, and the younger women. The best leaders are servant leaders, and servant leaders are teachable.

There are many examples of women who have a teachable spirit, including Mary and Martha, who were among Jesus' best friends. From the story in Luke 10:38–42, we are all quick to call Mary "teachable." It is Mary whose choice to listen gets praise from the Lord Jesus. She does everything she should do. When Jesus is around she listens to what He says. Martha is too distracted in her busyness to be teachable at that moment. You can almost hear the banging of the pots and pans, the heaving sighs as the last concoction is placed in the bowls. But before you are too hard on Martha, imagine the stress of fixing enough food, not just for Jesus and her siblings, but for the twelve extra guests Jesus always took with Him when He went out for dinner! Now imagine doing it without a modern stove or even a refrigerator. This woman is showing generous hospitality, and it has nearly killed her.

But turn over to John 12:1–8 where we drop in on a party thrown by Simon the ex-leper (another version of this story is given in Mark 14:1–9 that includes Simon's name). Martha served. And she served without a word of complaint. And you know that everyone in Bethany wished he was on that guest list! It is enough to know that the Twelve and Jesus and Lazarus and Simon were all there. And Martha served. Martha too had learned to be "teachable." Her course was longer since she had some rethinking to do about how Jesus prefers to be served. But she was teachable. She listened to the Savior when He scolded her ever so gently ("Martha, Martha . . ."), and she was never the same again. Oh, she once had tried to argue with Him about a theological issue just before He raised her brother from the dead. But even then, she listened finally after she argued.

Most of us like to think we are more like Mary—we listen first before we make mistakes—than Martha, whose impulsive choices of words made listening very hard. Either way, both Mary and Martha are teachable. The church needs women who are *teachable,* who when they simply trust and obey are blessed beyond measure and become role models for the rest of us.

A final need exists in terms of the kind of woman the church needs.

The Church Needs Women Who Are SENSITIVE

The spiritually sensitive women I have met are unconsciously sensitive. By that I mean they see a need and without examining, explaining, gossiping, or hesitating, they meet the need. They know exactly what the situation calls for. They hear the cry of the heart and provide the necessary nurturing women need. In their sensitivity, they make a safe place for a woman to cry, to confess, or to be comforted.

Most of the women who are praised in the New Testament share the quality of spiritual sensitivity. Mary herself echoed spiritual sensitivity to Gabriel as he announced the coming of the child who was to be the Messiah. She said, "I am the Lord's servant. . . . May it be to me as you have said" (Luke 1:38). Mary's sensitive heart to God's will was for the long journey, not the short trip. It put her in places where she didn't always know the answers. It led her to witness her own son on a bloody cross.

Anna—the feisty widow from the tribe of Asher—spent a lifetime at the temple worshiping, fasting, and praying (Luke 2:36–38). At the sight of the baby Jesus in Simeon's arms, she cried out about the child to all on the temple mount who would listen to her. To be overly sensitive is to be self-conscious. To be spiritually sensitive is to minister in ways God can use.

Another *S* belongs in this acronym. It is having a *sense of humor*. It is hard to work closely with any human being without a sense of humor. It is impossible to work in the family of God as women ministering to women without a good dose of humor. Humor is not sarcasm or laughing at another person's expense. But it is a great reliever of stress and is very good for your physical health.

CONCLUSION

If you plan to serve women in the local church with godly poise, you will need to develop those SMARTS. If you are a leader in your church, you will need to make sure you have women in your congregation who model these characteristics as a lifestyle.

The quality of the women in our churches is more important than any program we may start or any performance we may give. The size of the church is irrelevant. Most of the New Testament letters were written to churches of fewer than one hundred. Yet the church of Jesus Christ needs women who not only are smart but have SMARTS. Those women will live godly lives, will care more about developing their character than their charisma, will love God more than they love their own lives, and will boast not in their own power but the Master's.

Formal qualifications in training and theological preparation have their place. But there is a subtle danger in thinking they are adequate. I am grateful for the training I have received from my seminary experience, but it is an enhancement, not a replacement, for character qualifications and God-given gifts. This is not only true for women's ministries. It is true for all who seek to lead God's church in this generation.

THINK IT OVER

1. What women in your church model the characteristics represented by the acronym SMARTS?

2. Which of the qualities did you see modeled within your own home? How were they manifested?

3. Which of the qualities are most regularly modeled in the women who are leaders in your church?

THINK IT THROUGH

What characteristic can you see God developing in you? How is it being manifested?

> **S**piritual
> **M**ature
> **A**ble
> **R**esponsible
> **T**eachable
> **S**ensitive (with a sense of humor)

Pray for the Holy Spirit to transform you into a vessel of honor to be used by God.

NOTE

1. Miriam and Stuart Bundy, *Restoring the Soul: Experiencing God's Grace in Times of Crisis* (Chicago: Moody, 1999), 106.

Chapter Five

THE MANDATE
FOR MENTORING

"Mentoring is the process of developing a person to her maximum potential for the Lord Jesus Christ. The purpose of mentoring is character improvement and holiness, not perfection!"

ELIZABETH INRIG, *Mentoring Matters:*
A Bible Study on the Constellation Model of Mentoring

"A mentor may impact your life in a moment or for a long period of time; either way, the effect is for your good! . . . Mentoring is concerned about two primary areas of development. One is character and the other is attitude. Programs and structure are secondary."

"Women should minister to and nurture each other because we have a like spirit; we often 'feel' the same and can relate to one another."

SHELLY MALONEY, Women's Ministries

"I once had a friend named Grace. She was a former missionary at a Bible study I attended. My children were small and my husband worked long hours. When I shared my frustrations with her, she would pray with me and encourage me. I can't remember much of what she said, but I will never forget her compassion and unconditional love. She gave me hope. She also encouraged her children and grandchildren. She used to take trips to Ecuador to encourage wives who had husbands in prison."

"I come from a family of boys. I have seven brothers and love every one. But as I have grown from being a girl to a lady, I have found that women respond better to each other when we need to give or receive compassion and a particular kind of communication. Women are more likely to open up to other women and share needs."

Chapter Five

THE MANDATE FOR MENTORING

She did not know what it was called, but every time she did it, something important went on. One by one, the women would come. One
by one, she would show them how to mix the flour, sugar, and butter, all
the time kneading the dough. "As soon as the dough looks like a sponge,"
she would say, "it's ready to cut."

Sure enough, when she pulled the dough apart, it looked like the yel-
low sponge in the bathroom. Together my mother and the woman who had
come to see her rolled out the dough, cut it into shapes, and popped it in
the oven. Then, for the next thirty minutes, they would sit on the sofa and
"have a read." That was when my mother opened the Bible and read a text
to answer the young woman's questions. Sometimes they would pray.

Though my mother didn't know what it was called, she was mentoring. What she did know was that God had clearly explained how women
could become godly. She was simply obeying Titus 2:3–5. And as a little
girl, I watched my mother use her skill in making and baking shortbread
to build relationships with many younger women. But the skill was com-
bined with a conviction that she could train another generation for good
and God's glory.

In recent years there has been a resurgence of interest both in the secular and religious worlds in the idea of mentoring. Entire corporations have
recognized that though the young and the restless are energetic and visionary, they lack the practical experience that has weathered real life. They
need someone who has gone ahead of them to spend time with them, teaching, instructing, modeling, coaching them to make wise decisions on important matters. Huge mentoring programs have been established to make
sure the wisdom of the past is not lost for the future.

You may be interested to know that a movement like mentoring,
though it has become socially fashionable, does not have its inception in
culture. Its purposes are generated in the heart of God and are an essential

part of what He placed in Scripture centuries ago. For generations, the idea of mentoring has been a priority for the way God does things. It is the way He makes sure His children are passing on the torch of faith, spiritual wisdom, and skill in living to future generations of Christ followers.

The Obligation of the Mandate

We have been exploring the significance of women ministering to women in the context of the local church. We have heard women from around the world giving reasons why women should be ministering to women. When we study God's Word, we discover that God's Word confirms "women ministering to women" as a mandate. And at the heart of women serving women in the local church is the concept of mentoring. Before we define the term *mentoring,* it is crucial we understand the context in which the mandate is given to women.

The Great Challenge

We have already talked of things men and women share together as mandates from God for serving His church. First comes *the Great Call* to "follow Him" (John 10:3–5; 21:15–19). *The Great Commission* commands men and women to make disciples by baptizing and teaching Christ followers (Matthew 28:16–20). *The Great Commandment* commands us to love one another as the mark of discipleship (John 15:12). *The Great Charge* comes with the command to bear witness because of the power of the Holy Spirit who is *the Great Companion* (Acts 1:8). I call the mandate for women *the Great Challenge.* It commands women to do in the context of the local church what women alone can and should do. It does not include men because God has not asked men to minister to women in the way He has asked women to minister to women. He asks older women to model godliness so they can teach younger women. This is because women understand women, they share experiences unique to women, and it is one way God intends for others to honor His Word (Titus 2:3–5).

The Context of the Mandate

In order to properly interpret Scripture and, in this case, extract principles for how women best minister to women in the local church, it is important to understand the context in which the command to women is given.

Titus is one of three books in the New Testament known as Pastoral Letters. They are known as pastorals because they include instructions for church leaders so they will know how people should conduct themselves in God's household. The letters are written to two individuals, Timothy and Titus, both of whom were left by Paul to shepherd local churches. Timothy was left in Ephesus and Titus was at Crete.

Paul's reason for leaving Titus in Crete and then writing him is so he would "straighten out" things that were left undone in the church after Paul left Crete. He was to appoint men to be elders who qualified primarily by their blameless life and behavior, as husbands and fathers, and in their commitment to the apostles' teaching (Titus 1:6–9). Those men were to encourage others by sound doctrine and refute those who opposed it (Titus 1:10–16).

Paul addresses Titus personally as to his responsibility as a shepherd of this church. His primary role as shepherd/pastor is to teach sound doctrine to the local church in Crete (Titus 2:1). Specifically, Titus is to make sure he focuses on two groups. The older men are to be taught to be temperate, worthy of respect, self-controlled, and sound in faith, love, and endurance. The older women are to be taught in the same intentional way Titus teaches the older men. He is to teach them to be reverent in the way they live, not to be gossips, and not to be addicted to much wine. In turn, the older women are to teach what is good so they can train the younger women to love their husbands and their children. When they live in such a way with their husbands and children, people will not malign the Word of God.

After giving instructions for teaching women, Paul goes on to give specific instructions for young men (Titus 2:6–8) and slaves (vv. 9–10). The elders and pastors preach *sound doctrine* (truth that brings health). They teach sound doctrine to the older men, older women, younger men, and slaves. The older women take what they have been taught in the public meetings of the church, apply it to their own lives, and mingle it with the skills they have finessed. Then they are ready to teach the younger women what God has instructed them to teach.

The Definition of Mentoring

The process we have described is one way of describing the process of mentoring. It is a catchall word that includes the informal and formal investment of one woman into another woman's life. It includes such words as discipling, teaching, coaching, sponsoring, modeling, guiding and is different from *a program* in mentoring. To begin from the same place, we will define *mentoring:*

> Mentoring *is the process of developing a person to her maximum potential for the Lord Jesus Christ. The object of mentoring is improvement and holiness, not perfection. A* mentor *is someone committed to help another grow so* that the process of maturing continues for a lifetime *and helps her* realize her God-given purpose and achieve her God-given life goals.

The Dimensions of Mentoring

True mentoring is concerned about two primary areas of development. One is character and the other is attitude. The program or structure of mentoring is always secondary. According to Paul in Philippians 2:1–4, the impact character and attitude have on mentoring is fueled by humility. It is this aspect of mentoring that qualifies an older woman to invest spiritually in the lives of other women. Mentoring may be a relationship that started serendipitously, but it is an intentional relationship because you're concerned about people younger than you. It is an irresistible relationship.

True mentoring is a lifestyle. That means while the "event" type program of mentoring may meet the need of a group of women for a limited time, the potential for "lifestyle" mentoring is unlimited. It happens whenever a mentor is aware of her ability to invest for good in the life of another woman and sometimes even when she is not aware of it. The everyday process of affecting another woman's life for good is open to any woman at any time. Most women appreciate the gracious input of older women into their lives.

This was brought to my attention a few years ago when our church made a choice to intentionally match older women and younger women together for mutual nourishing. Of the seventy-five women who came to fill out the profile we had created, all but one said she wanted an older woman to mentor her! We didn't have that many "older" women. We have since disbanded our contrived matches and instead have laced every one of our ministries to women with a mentoring component. It is the backbone of the way we arrange our small groups in Bible study. We never put the young women together; they are mingled with the older women and all of those in between. That is because as you look at the models of Scripture and examine the effect of others on your life, you recognize there is rarely the separation of ages in ministry. Every stage of a woman's life becomes a means by which she can encourage others regardless of their age. When women in ministry spend time only with those in their own age group, they miss the richness of lives well-lived.

Principles for Mentoring

Mentoring Is for Qualified Women. Paul, in his words to the older women in Crete who are going to begin to teach or nourish the younger women in the church, points out clearly the primary qualification for mentoring: It is an attitude of reverence, a state of mind that is suitable to holiness. He says the older women in Crete are to be reverent "in the way they live." It is irrelevant to Paul that Cretans are reputed to be liars (Titus 1:10–13)! He expects the older Christian woman to live like a woman engaged in sacred duties, not like the culture in which she grew up. Reverence in living means "behavior suitable to a sacred person" and implies the attitude someone has when he or she is set apart for holy purposes. Reverential behavior requires two things from an older woman: that she does not engage in gossip or behave like a slanderer passing judgment on others and that she must not overindulge in or be enslaved to wine. The union of these two negatives may suggest a close connection between a loose tongue and intoxicating drink.[1]

This attitude of reverence before God is addressed repeatedly in the Old Testament and specifically in the book of Proverbs where the writer says the fear of God is the beginning of wisdom. The Proverbs 31 woman is known not as one who is focused on external charm or beauty so much as she is a woman who fears the Lord and should be praised for that (Proverbs 31:30). David says that fear of the Lord is not automatic but that it must be taught (Psalm 34:11–14). Just because a woman is a Christ follower does not mean she has a humble, reverent heart. The fear of the Lord is a learned attitude that one believer teaches another: "Come, my children, listen to me; I will teach you the fear of the LORD" (Psalm 34:11). Titus says older women are to be those who have learned reverence so that they can teach it to younger women.

If you are young, do not make the mistake of thinking that you will wait until you are forty or fifty to learn to fear the Lord. Everyone is older than someone, so start now by learning the fear of the Lord and modeling it to a younger woman under your wing. Proverbs 20:5 and 27:17 confirm that learning, modeling, and teaching reverence is a wise choice.

Mentoring Lies at the Heart of Women's Ministries. Paul moves now to the positive pattern that Titus can expect the older women to follow: They should make a commitment to "teach what is good" because they have rejected the wrong use of their tongues and their appetites. The role older women take when they teach what is good by personal word and example fulfills God's purposes for maintaining spiritual health in the next generation of women. The older women are called to teach what is morally good, noble, and attractive. They are to teach it as an extension of their character. They are to take seriously the command to teach what is good, because what they teach affects the health of the relationships in the home and in the church. The word "teacher in good" does not simply refer to formal instruction, but rather the advice and encouragement older women can give privately by word and example.[2]

Recently a woman whose husband serves in a very significant leadership role in the Christian community said to me during a mentoring seminar: "I have never been mentored by anyone! In fact, I can't think of any woman who has intentionally mentored me." If you have said this or felt this, let me remind you that mentoring does not only happen because you "do" a program or have been matched with a woman for a period of time, although mentoring may include that. But it is observing godly women who motivate you to follow the Lord more closely. Sometimes it is being influenced for good in a single moment. Some of my most important mentors are women I have never met personally, but as I have read their stories (such as Amy Carmichael of India or Lilias Trotter of Algeria), their lives have burned a passion in my heart to know God like they knew God. They prompted me to make changes in the way I thought about my Christian life. They are my mentors. Mentoring can be serendipitous as well as planned. So, if you think you have never been mentored, put a blank piece of paper in front of you and write your age in increments of five or ten years down the left side (ages 1–5, 6–10, and so on up until the present). Then go back in your mind over the past to all the women who taught you at least one thing about living wisely or having a godly lifestyle. You will find yourself delighting in the way God has put women in your life at specific times to teach you what you could never have learned without them. And probably you will realize you have been mentored.

Mentoring Focuses on Training. Paul leaves Titus with a clear understanding of what he must instruct the older women to teach the younger women in the local church. The seven characteristics both describe the women who teach what is good and are those they commend to the younger women. They do this through the means of *training*, a word that means to "school" in the lessons of sobriety and self-control.[3] Before we examine the substance of the mentoring mandate, three things worth noticing are implicit in these verses. First, the mandate is not entrusted to the older men or younger men or even Pastor Titus. It is a mandate for godly older women. Second, the mandate is not given as a charge to women in the church in general. It is given to those who qualify by their godly lifestyle. Chronological age alone does not qualify a woman as godly. Spiritual age does not qualify a woman as mature. Only the practice of faithful godliness qualifies an older woman to train a younger woman. I have known older women who call themselves Christians who are bitter, do not love their husbands, do not speak to their adult children, are careless with their tongues, and are addicted to food, to shopping, to collecting things, to a variety of distractions. They disqualify themselves by their choices. Third, the older women who should be training younger women are those who respect Titus's teaching of sound doctrine. They are faithful followers of church leaders.

The seven characteristics Paul commends are stated in pairs. If you are a godly older woman, this is what you must teach the younger women in your local church.

The first pair is this: Teach them to love their husband and love their children. The emphasis is on the idea of "devotion." The woman of God is devoted to her husband. She is devoted to her children (Titus 2:4). The word Paul uses for "love" is *phileo*, the family love that implies warm affection (literally husband-loving, children-loving) that is at the heart of a godly home. It is this love that makes for spiritual health in the local church.

The second pair is this: Teach them to be self-controlled and pure (Titus 2:5). Self-control is a characteristic of Christ followers in the New Testament Epistles. It is evidence of the Spirit's presence in a believer's life and is the standing duty of the believer. It is an evidence of the fruit of the Spirit (Galatians 5:23). It is expected of those who are children of the day (1 Thessalonians 5:6, 8; 1 Peter 1:13), and it is a mark of those who qualify for elders (1 Timothy 3:2) as well as godly men in general (Titus 2:2). It is a necessary quality for those who are not anxious but who seek to pray (1 Peter 4:7; 5:8). In a time when greed and affluence abound, godly women must learn to have self-control. The partner to self-control is the characteristic of purity, which implies the women in the church choose to be chaste or pure of heart in all their conduct—another stark contrast to the times in which we live.

The third set of characteristics carries with it very practical matters. The godly older woman is to teach the younger woman to be busy at home (Titus 2:5). The implication is as mundane as the fact of "working at home" or "housekeeping," those things that are part of everyday life for the woman in the home. In a Jewish household the married woman had to grind flour, bake, launder, cook, nurse children, make the beds, spin wool, and keep the house. She was also responsible for hospitality and the care of guests. First Timothy 5:9–10 confirms these activities as characteristic of noble women.[4] The woman who willingly accepts the activities of the home leaves no room for idleness, another reminder of the virtuous woman in Proverbs 31:17, 19. This characteristic is expected of younger widows as well, who may be tempted to be idle and busybodies (1 Timothy 5:13–15), giving Satan ammunition for slandering God's people.

The second part of managing the home well is the importance of doing it in a spirit of kindness. A long time ago now, when our children were little, on a snowy Monday morning in Calgary, Canada, I was hurrying one of my children out the door to school. As a pastor's family, Sundays were always busy, filled with people and invariably with guests for lunch. As I shooed my child out the door, I heard the sound of a voice ask, "Mummy, why can't you treat us like company?" Why couldn't I just be kind?

To be kind. What does it matter if you are organized perfectly or you cross everything off your to-do list at night if you have not been kind? Who cares if you have shown grace to the church people if you have been cranky with your family? The woman in Proverbs 31 chooses kindness as a characteristic of her life: "The teaching of kindness is on her tongue" (v. 26 NASB). Why be kind as you manage your home? Because the God whom we serve is immeasurably kind. Paul says in Romans 2:4 that it is His kindness to us that leads us to repentance, not His annoyance or stingy spirit. It is His kindness that gives me the grace I need to understand what kind of God He is. The same is true in the home of Christ followers. The mother who manages her home and remains kind is a woman to be praised. Kindness to the family does not preclude discipline or correction. It simply offers a place of grace in which to grow and a place of safety in which to fail so that at the end of the day, our family members know they are loved.

The final characteristic of the godly woman who is training young women to model a godly lifestyle is the *S* word. There is no time to discuss in detail the impact of the concept of submission, the voluntary coming under or voluntary acceptance of the leadership of her husband. It is enough to say the idea has come into hard times with the feminist movement and with men who continue to model a chauvinistic attitude toward women. The characteristic of loving my husband does not remove the responsibility I have to yield to his headship. As he leads in love the way Paul describes in Ephesians 5:28, my joy is to respond in submission to this leadership as my act of respect (Ephesians 5:22).

One answer to an anticipatory question, whether men and women are both called to submission: Submission is a many splendored thing. In Ephesians 5:21, it is asked of both men and women. In declaring our spiritual equality before God as Galatians 3:28 describes, Paul does not exclude the functional differences between man and woman, husband and wife in the home or the local church. The joy of the godly woman is to complement her husband just as any instrument would harmonize with the lead violin in the orchestra. Equality of value between man and woman is without dispute in Scripture. So is being complementary yet different in function.

THE REASON FOR THE MANDATE

The New International Version of the Scripture repeatedly uses a phrase that should help us as we study the Bible. It is the phrase "so that." It follows certain instructions, commands, and explanations with a reason that will convince the student of the value of the instruction. In this case, the mandate for mentors is clear: Older godly women are to teach younger women what is good. Lest you read the verses and remain unconvinced about the substance of this mandate, Paul assures Titus there is a bigger purpose than just a happy family or a healthy local church. He says the motivation for and goal of this instruction is "so that" no one will malign the Word of God.

Herein lies the greatest power available to women in the church today. Simple obedience to God's ways produces a life-transforming effect on those who observe this process. This final promise or clause relates to all seven commendations and becomes the passionate purpose for which an older woman will be godly and a younger woman will be obedient. When women in the local church ignore God's mandate, nonbelievers will malign the gospel, criticize the church, and discredit the value of Christian principles. But when older women model these characteristics and train the younger women to imitate them, they protect the revelation of God as given in Scripture. As they live discreet and wholesome lives, they model lives that do not hinder the rapid spread and effectiveness of God's Word.

THE POWER OF THE MANDATE

If you are a Christ follower who has a passion to obey God's Word, here is where you can start. First, if you are married, start in your own home as you model the spirit of Titus 2 before your husband, your sons, and your daughters. Then as you become credible in the way you live your life, women younger than you will observe your conduct. In a single moment when you least expect, your life may impact theirs for good and the glory of God. That is what mentoring is all about. The power is in obedience to the Word. You are not being asked to explain why God asks this of you. You are only asked to obey with joy. When you take hold of this mandate, the eternal and inevitable happens: God's Word is honored and not maligned.

THINK IT OVER

Lifestyle Mentoring: Take a look at your own life as you answer these questions.

1. Who have been your mentors? Use the definition in this chapter (p. 78) as your measuring stick.

2. Whose life have you influenced?

3. Recall some of the Bible characters whose lives were affected and changed by godly mentors in the Old Testament and in the New Testament. What was most significant in their stories?

4. What things have you seen happen during a time when one woman affected another woman's life for good?

THINK IT THROUGH

If you are part of a mentoring program, the following reminders may help clarify some things for you.

1. Mentoring is a transitional relationship. It may last anywhere from nine months to two years. If you choose to use a set program, make sure you set a time for closure as you begin any partnership with another woman.

2. Mentoring is a personal relationship. It is not an official relationship so much as it is a match in the best sense of the word.

3. Mentoring is a diverse relationship. A character mentor is personal; "who she is" is important in terms of character and attitudes. A role mentor is more practical; "what she does" is significant. Over a lifetime you will need a variety of mentors.

4. Mentoring is a demanding relationship. The essential requirement of any mentoring is maturity. Mentoring is not intended to be therapy. Mentoring is being godly yourself so you can invest in another person's life.

5. Mentoring is a vibrant relationship. There is no canned approach to mentoring. Rather, it grows out of the needs and questions of the one being mentored. Bible study and discipleship should not be replaced by a mentoring relationship, only enhanced by it.

6. Mentoring requires the investment of significant moments. Whether planned or spontaneous, every moment is significant when those you mentor see Jesus in your life.

NOTES

1. D. Edmond Hiebert, *Titus* in *The Expositor's Bible Commentary* (Grand Rapids: Zondervan, 1978), 438.
2. Quoted in Fritz Rienecker and Cleon Rogers, ed. *Linguistic Key to the Greek New Testament* (Grand Rapids: Zondervan, 1976), 654.
3. Hiebert, *Expositor's Bible Commentary, Titus,* 438.
4. *Linguistic Key to the Greek New Testament,* 654.

Chapter Six

WOMEN ARE
UNIQUELY WOMEN

*"I really appreciate finding out that I am not the only woman going through that
struggle, that I'm not strange or abnormal and I'm not going to come apart.
Another woman has 'been there and done that' and God helped her through it as
He will help me."*

MARY EPP, Trinity Women's Ministries

*"We share the bond of being 'female' and that brings a unique perspective on
life!"*

*"There is a special bond between women that is gender related and born of the
heart. Women can cut through the superficial exteriors that we show each other.
That is hard to appreciate sometimes!"*

*"It is mainly women in my life who have taught me how important it is that
when I have publicly failed, to take it with grace and poise which speaks volumes
more than pristine, polished, perfect performances!"*

*"Your beauty should not come from outward adornment, such as braided hair and
the wearing of gold jewelry and fine clothes. Instead, it should be that of your
inner self, the unfading beauty of a gentle and quiet spirit, which is of great worth
in God's sight."*

1 Peter 3:3–4

Chapter Six

WOMEN ARE UNIQUELY WOMEN

*D*uring a visit to Australia, I made a wonderful discovery: a delightful bakery that served early morning lattes and delicious fresh breads. One morning on my usual early morning walk, I stopped by an hour later than normal only to find nothing was ready. No scones. No cinnamon swirls. Just lattes. As I was paying for the coffee, the lady serving me explained the problem.

"The owner is a bit behind this morning. His wife had a baby last night."

Looking past the doorway I could see a man covered with flour and beaming with pride.

"What did you have?" I asked.

"My wife had a baby!"

"But what kind of baby did you have?" I repeated to him, wondering whether he could give me more details.

"My wife had a live baby!"

Hmm. Not exactly the answer I was looking for. I wondered how I could clarify the question when the woman at the front of the store helped me out.

"She wants to know the details: Is it a boy or girl?"

"Of course, I should have known that's what you meant. It's a girl!"

Women's ministry—in any church—isn't a complicated matter if you begin with the understanding that *men and women share humanity in common, but we are different from each other.* Our uniqueness as women—how we think, how we react, how we feel—sets us apart from men.

The example of my conversation with the Australian owner of the bakery is a silly one, but it happens often. Men like headlines; women like the details. I would have loved to know the weight, the length, whether the baby had lots of hair, how long the labor was, and what they named the little girl. I was lucky to find out that the baby was a girl.

On a regular basis, I ask women *why* women should be ministering to women. In one thousand responses, every third reason is this: because women are uniquely like each other. We are genetically different from men. We are female in our makeup and understand each other in ways men do not understand us or each other.

Even those women who do not share responsibility in women's ministries admit to needing women in their lives. They simply prefer to have them by choice and in smaller quantities! The truth is that women are uniquely created "female," the idea of which goes back to the beginning of all things.

THE ANCIENT RECORD

The Bible is God's self-revelation. When God speaks, He speaks the truth to us. He does not lie about who He is or what He does. To understand how His truth intersects with our lives, we must understand that it is carried by the stories in the Bible of real individuals living in nations and cities that existed on the earth. People in the stories are not that different from you and me, who meet the one true God and His Son, Jesus Christ. The individual stories combine together over time and carry the truth of God's plans for man to their final purpose: to glorify Him in all things. We noticed that because the Bible is a literary book, the truth that is carried by stories is also symbolized by pictures, figures of speech, and parables. Consequently, we can say with confidence that the Bible is a supernatural book of literature to which we apply the ordinary laws of English grammar (or the language in which it is written). It is written into a specific historical context to people in specific geographical places, and although it reflects the cultures of the times, the cultures do not determine its truth. It is theological in nature and is ultimately a book about God and His purposes for mankind.

The Uniqueness of the Woman

God describes His preparation of the woman and Moses records it in Genesis 2:18–25. Moses paints a clear picture of men and women, husbands and wives before the Fall. The "ideals" set forth in these verses describe the perfect marriage relationship. Catch the flavor of the Garden of Eden as you watch God prepare this companion for Adam.

Adam has spent a long time with the animals. Day after day he has looked at each one. God gave him authority to name them. In naming the animals, Adam makes a statement of his leadership under God and authority over the animals. Now they have come and gone: long necks, furry coats, flapping ears, stubby tails, some moving with ease and others awkward and wobbly. All are gone now and without exception are found inadequate as a personal, intimate companion. We have no idea how long it took for Adam to name the animals. We only know that God, foreseeing Adam's aloneness, says "alone" is not good (Genesis 2:18). God determines to find a "suitable helper" to complement this lack. It is her difference to Adam that qualifies the companion chosen by God for Adam.

The story is old but important. God puts the man to sleep and removes a rib from his side. From the rib, God makes a "complement" for Adam, and she is one of a kind. Adam's whoop, "At last! Bone of my bones, flesh of my flesh!" is well deserved. After staring at hundreds of animals unlike him, he is delighted to meet this lady well suited for him in a way no animal ever was. We do not know how long this idyllic state lasts. We can only imagine the sheer joy of companionship and purity of sexual love enjoyed by these two. It is an intense moment of beauty as man and woman—similar in substance (dust, bone) and different in shape and purpose—come together in more excellent harmony than the best trained orchestra under a canopy of stars. It is for this lasting commitment to each other that the Lord God states: "A man will leave his father and mother and be united to his wife, and they will become one flesh" (Genesis 2:24).

Equal in Value, Different in Function

There is no doubt from these verses as to the equal value of man and woman. The woman is both equal to and adequate for the man. She is equal in her personhood and dignity, and the man admires her value (Genesis 2:23). There is no trace of chauvinism in this relationship nor desire to dominate or control. Both are asked to be fruitful and multiply and subdue the earth (Genesis 1:28). This statement of equality is repeated in the New Testament in Galatians 3:26–28 long after the fall of man. In the context of warning his readers against turning back to the Law of Moses (where the woman had no rights except through her husband), Paul will later remind the Galatians that when it comes to a relationship of faith, there is no hierarchy. There is only one category: Men and women alike need salvation.

There is also no doubt from this passage that Adam is prepared for leadership by naming the animals. Now he names his bride: "She shall be called 'woman' [Hebrew: *ishshah*], for she was taken out of man [Hebrew: *ish*]. But she is also different to Adam as intended by God. It is her very difference that enables her to complement him and free him from his "aloneness."

After the Fall, Adam and Eve share equally in death. Both die spiritually; both know God's personal curse against their sin. Both are promised pain in the very areas they would have known joy. But we will never understand the wonder of our difference until we understand this: Their equality in worth does not include the interchangeability of their roles. Adam will always be held responsible for the chaos in the garden, a fact that Moses records in Genesis 3:9: "The LORD God called to the man, 'Where are you?'" Paul confirms it in Romans 5:17: ("By the trespass of the one man, death reigned through that one man." Adam is responsible to God, and Eve will always be held responsible in relationship to Adam (1 Timothy 2:9–15). The man is asked, as the leader, to give an account of the situation to God. The woman is not given Adam's responsibility. She is not asked to give the final answer. She has a different role. In fact, if you eavesdrop on the conversation Eve had with the Serpent, you will see where she was deceived: in relationship to God's words. If you eavesdrop on the conversation Eve had with Adam, *you do not hear her ask for advice*—she did not ask him what he thought—*and Adam's silence thunders!* He did not say a word. He ate the apple with his eyes wide open.

Women are equal to men but not interchangeable with men. It is as true in the physical realm as it is in the spiritual realm. But it is our *difference from men* that positions us to minister to women, not our similarities. And it is being the God-intended complement to man that keeps the differences from becoming a detriment to the health of the church. Differences that set apart women as unique are the basis for harmony and rapport in the church.

THE RECENT FINDINGS

It is interesting to visit different restaurants and notice the labels they place on their restrooms. Some will say "Gentlemen" and "Ladies." Others list "Men" and "Women." In an old private girls' school in which I was speaking in Sydney, the doors said "Male" and "Female." Obviously a statement from the past.

When distinction between the sexes is blurred, a mind-set that has been around for a long time (see Deuteronomy 22:5 and Romans 1:21–27), an understanding of female is important. No one who lived in the last half of the previous century is ignorant of the effect of the feminist movement. All of us have given some thought at some point to the question of what it means to be a woman in this generation. Although the feminist movement has exposed injustices in the working world and political process, things for which I am thankful, it has done a disservice to what it means to be a woman. In spite of the sweeping cultural changes, the replacement roles have not proved to be satisfying or permanent. You may change the traditional roles of women, but you cannot remove the genetic code "female" from a woman's body!

Countless books have been written on the differences of men and women. Some address our different communication styles (*You Just Don't Understand* by Deborah Tannen). Others, like John Gray's *Men Are from Mars; Women Are from Venus,* make the differences between us clear. Faith Popcorn, in *EVEolution,* confirms not only a biological difference between men and women but that the biological difference determines the way a woman shops, spends, connects, lives, and chooses.[1]

The important thing here is to understand that women are uniquely women. So, how are women uniquely women? Let me suggest three general answers, many of which were repeated by the one thousand women I asked the question, "Why should women minister to women?" Let's look at the three most common answers.

Women Understand Women

Whether it is an intuitive gift or good observation skills, women generally understand not only what is being expressed by another woman but how it feels.

"I can begin to describe a situation with my daughter and my friend's eyes do not immediately glaze over. She nods affirmingly and seems to feel exactly how I feel. She understands me! Someone understands me! I think I can even get through the day if I know one other woman understands how hard it is to deal with what I am dealing with."

"Women don't need a Ph.D. to know where another woman is coming from emotionally. We came from the same planet and therefore have a unique perspective on each other's needs."

Women should minister to women because they speak the same heart language.

Women Miss You When You're Not There

Women value bonding, and being together in a group means the group isn't complete unless you are there.

"I joined the mothers' group because I needed to know others had two-year-olds like mine! And then my child was sick and I had to stay home. The leaders called to see what happened, if my car had broken down or I was sick and needed a meal brought in! They missed me! That made me feel wanted and valued."

Women should minister to women because women notice when they're not there.

Women Share Similar Life Experiences

In February 1991, I sat in a doctor's office in Medical City in Dallas. I was waiting for him to give me the result of a mammogram. I was busy redecorating his office although I am no interior decorator. The hospital-green sink was cracked, the flooring needed to be replaced, and I thought he could do with a new calligrapher for his name on his degree. Cancer was the last thing I was thinking about that day.

When Dr. Aaronoff walked in with my X rays under his arm, he proceeded to show me the suspicious growths. By the end of the week, the biopsy came back positive and the cancerous breast was confirmed: I would need a mastectomy as soon as possible. It is a long time ago now, but I remember sitting quietly, alone, saying nothing, wondering exactly what would happen to me. Whether I would live or die, see my children raised and married. It was then that the Holy Spirit brought a verse to my mind, though at the time I didn't know the reference. "You died, and your life is now hidden with Christ in God" (Colossians 3:3). I later discovered it was tucked away in the context of the command to "set your mind on things above, not on earthly things." The verse didn't change the diagnosis, nor did the prayer of the elders and the anointing of oil on my body. But it quieted my heart at a very stressful moment. That week, I had the surgery and I am still alive, praise God! For many years I have told that story to women where I have spoken and invariably, at the end of the talk, a handful of women will come and thank me for talking about my fears, my need to trust. Sometimes I talk about a depression I went through or difficult ministry times. Always I discover other women have been there too. We have things in common that ease the burden of the journey because a sister in Christ has walked a similar road.

I once asked a young woman in our church to speak about her struggle to get pregnant. She spoke of her longing for a child. She told us that no matter how hard she worked, her career as a dentist could not fill her empty heart. She went on to describe the marvelous way God opened up a door for her and her husband to adopt a baby boy. She went on to give birth to another healthy baby boy. Looking around the room, I saw women weeping, and I knew they could understand her hurt and her joy. But I will never forget the words she said that helped me realize an important lesson in all of this pain: We are women first before we take on any role God may give to us. My friend said it well: "I had to stop thinking that my value and worth was in becoming a mother. I had to start thanking God for making me a woman. My worth is not related primarily to my role. My worth is directly related to the fact that as a woman, I am made in the image of God. I began to see that if I say, 'I need this or that' before I can be happy, I will never be happy or content with how and who God made me."

Women are uniquely "women." That is our basic connection. We share the same genetic code. For women who are Christ followers, we share the life of Christ, and the understanding only grows.

WOMEN'S UNIQUE INFLUENCE ON OTHER WOMEN FOR GOOD

As a postscript to my experience with cancer, God taught me that my greatest need is to find Him as my grand and certain comfort. But there is an added blessing when women experience situations that other women alone can understand. He sends one of His own daughters. Someone who, because she has found comfort in Him, can give away the comfort she received (2 Corinthians 1). He taught me this through someone who knew Him better than I did.

Surgery for my breast cancer was on Friday. I went home Saturday. Sunday, the busiest day of our week as a pastor's family, was quiet for me that week. What I didn't know was that one of the elders' wives, Gladys, had arranged with Gary to come and sit with me. I will never forget how softly she slipped into our bedroom, gave me a kiss, and assured me she would sit quietly. She prayed a short prayer while I fell in and out of sleep. At one point, she said: "I've brought some verses on three-by-five cards to encourage you. When I battled cancer, they were my lifeline!"

What a gift God brought to me that day. Glad didn't come to preach. She didn't come to help me understand the mystery of pain and disease. She didn't suggest a quick cure or try to explain to me why I had cancer. No one ever really can. Instead, she let God speak *for her to me* in the same way He had spoken *to her* when she was fighting cancer—from His Word. With a humble spirit and because she knew my fears, disappointment, and hope as a woman who'd gone through my pain, she understood my need. She brought me back home that Sunday morning to God—the triune God of the world whose Son is my Savior and whose Spirit is my comforter and teacher. I'd known Him to be faithful before. But Glad knew I needed a fresh glimpse of Him for that day. This year, nine years later, Glad went home to be with the Lord, ending her battle with cancer. I will never forget her act of kindness. She took me back to the God I loved. I will always be convinced that as a woman, she uniquely cared. She met my needs that day in the way others couldn't. Her impact on my heart will last a lifetime.

There are hundreds of situations in which women are uniquely gifted to minister to women. For me, it was the experience of breast cancer. There is no substitute for a woman who has been where I am. But even my friends who had not had cancer could come into this very private world and lift me up. One friend, Shirley, came to my home and prayed faithfully with me throughout the tests, the surgery, and the months that followed. Another friend, Martha, flew down from Canada to take care of me the week following surgery. Others according to their gifts and personal sensitivity, women who believed in the God of all comfort, comforted me in my time of need.

What Is Unique About You?

In chapter 9, I use the acronym "DESIGN" to help women find where they fit in the scheme of the gifts of their local church. As you look back over your life, you will remember that God is sovereign, He is gracious, and He wastes nothing, including the important *experiences* in your life: the highs, the lows, the things God uses to teach you the most important lessons in life. Before you dismiss the things the sovereign Lord has allowed to come into your life, see each one as an entrustment from God for comfort. As you lift the times of disappointment or grief up to the Lord or as you repent of the sins of your youth, you discover His redeeming power in your life. He can use even the ugliest sins, when they are abandoned, as a means of serving others. Even the hardest times become tools of encouragement in the hands of the one who knows the faithfulness of God.

So what is unique about your experience? In what experiences have you been forced to go to God alone for faithful and loyal support? Where have you learned God? What has He done for you that is worth declaring to the women in your life who need a word from Him? Think of the ways in which you could have proved Him: singleness, PMS, a difficult marriage, a barren womb, a handicapped child, an unwanted pregnancy, child rearing, loneliness, cancer in any number of female organs, postpartum depression, menopause, and experience from many womanly experiences. The fact of shared experiences is not so important as the way we learn God through these times. It was Gladys's humble walk with the Lord that put her in a position to encourage me. God's purpose for these unique experiences of life is not to be wasted in our lives. Nor should they make us angry. Peter's words help us here when he says, "These [trials] have come so that your faith . . . may be proved genuine and may result in praise, glory and honor when Jesus Christ is revealed" (1 Peter 1:7). The purpose is that we would be the bearers of comfort to the body of Christ. Paul teaches this marvelous ministry in words from 2 Corinthians 1:3–7.

> *Praise be to the God and Father of our Lord Jesus Christ, the Father of compassion and the God of all comfort, who comforts us in all our troubles, so that we can comfort those in any trouble with the comfort we ourselves have received from God. For just as the sufferings of Christ flow over into our lives, so also through Christ our comfort overflows. If we are distressed, it is for your comfort and salvation; if we are comforted, it is for your comfort, which produces in you patient endurance of the same sufferings we suffer. And our hope for you is firm, because we know that just as you share in our sufferings, so also you share in our comfort.*

Think of it. You are a woman with unique experiences. These experiences, events, occurrences, and happenings, beginning with your family of origin and leading up to the city where you live and the job where God has placed you, from the education you have to the diseases you have or don't have—all these experiences have been allowed into your life by the sovereign Lord of the universe. They are assignments God has entrusted to you as a source of comfort for others. The truth according to Paul is that if you have sought the comfort of God through these times, you are qualified to comfort those in any trouble with the comfort you have received from God. For women who have proved God during tough times, the potential for spiritual health among women in the local church is remarkable. The challenge is clear: God's primary means of comfort for women in the body of Christ is the proven comfort of God in every situation. In case you think you are alone in your distress, read on in 2 Corinthians 1:8–9 to see what Paul faced. "We were under great pressure, far beyond our ability to endure, so that we despaired even of life. . . . But this happened that we might not rely on ourselves but on God, who raises the dead."

Women Share Stage-of-Life Experiences

Some specific stages in life become the unique things women share. Marriage is one of them. If God should grant you the gift of marriage, this is a role that you share with thousands of women. The example of the godly older women in the church makes this a primary tool for understanding women's unique needs. Since every woman who is a wife is older than someone, begin your own study of your marriage, your husband, and God's Word. That way, you will be ready to answer women married fewer years than you on what it means to love your husband and know his love language.[2] In this regard, I would love to hear from Peter's wife, who Paul says in 1 Corinthians 9:3–6 went with him on his ministry trips as he shepherded the churches of God. I would like to know the things she shared with other wives. As a pastor's wife, she would have had to adjust to an outgoing, committed, and zealous Christian husband! It is interesting that it is her husband who confirms the fact that wives may have in common the experience of a "disobedient husband" and how she can cope with it (1 Peter 3:1–7). One note of caution: Husband bashing is never edifying. It is one of the few rules we have for our Bible study groups.

Related to mutual encouragement in marriage is an interesting statistic. Most women married today will outlive their husbands. That means women more than men will face the challenge of being left alone in old age. Women therefore possess a unique ability to minister to widows, another important aspect of church ministry at a time when the graying of America is a reality.

Women Share the Same Role Experiences

No one attends a meeting of preschool mothers without realizing that as mothers, women speak the same heart language! Entire organizations have sprung up across the world bringing mothers together. Many times it is for commiseration—the comparing of childlike behaviors with others in similar straits. It is good news to know that your children are normal when they say "no" at two and that "this too shall pass." Young mothers need what the Bible says they need: older mothers who have grown in faith as they have brought up their children (see 1 Timothy 5:10). In fact, it is not possible for young mothers to keep a healthy perspective apart from having older godly women in their church who are mothers or surrogate mothers encourage them to mother well. It is true that God gives some women the role of mother, but He graciously includes those who are "aunts" who have a valuable womanly role in children's and mothers' lives.

Many years ago, a single woman cared for my husband and his two brothers when they were young children. She headed up the nursery in the church he attended and supported the mothers and their little ones in ways too many to list. To this day, Gary praises this "mother in Israel." Though she never had any biological children, she had a heart to nurture both the mothers and their children. Praise God if you have women like Grace McPhee who nurture from their God-given instinct and experience as wisely and kindly as those who are biological mothers.

Two wonderful examples of the unique and mutual understanding between mothers is told in the New Testament. Paul applauds Lois, the grandmother, and Eunice, the mother, of Timothy for the consistent way they have worked together to teach Timothy the Scriptures. At this point in history, the Old Testament was their only Bible. The lesson is clear: As a mother, your primary focus for investing in your eternal future and leaving a legacy is in your daughters. Once they become mothers, there is an added joy and responsibility of sharing (with boundaries!) the parenting experience.

The second example is powerful. When Mary hears that she has been chosen to be the mother of our Lord, she leaves in haste to spend three months with her old cousin Elizabeth (Luke 1:26–56). How I would love to have crouched behind the curtain as these two women, surprised by the grand grace of God to them, share this experience of motherhood. The text never says whether Elizabeth, barren all her life until now, gives birth to John the Baptist before Mary leaves. I hope Mary was there as Elizabeth went into labor. What a wonderful experience it would have been to learn how to have a baby—especially since we know on the night of Jesus' birth, only Joseph aided her. Perhaps she was comforted by the cry of the baby John in those Judean hills. Just as John's birth was the sign that God always keeps His promises, so the Lord Jesus' birth fulfilled Gabriel's words: "For nothing is impossible with God!" (Luke 1:37).

Women Should Minister to Women Because They Are Uniquely Women

Why should women minister to women? At the heart of why women should minister to women is the fact that we take seriously *whose we are:* We belong to God, the master craftsman. We must value God's heart purposes for us. At the heart of why women should minister to women is the fact that we rejoice in *how God has skillfully created us:* female, with the signature of God upon the shape of our bodies and the webbing of our brains. We must value His work.

At the heart of why women should minister to women is the fact that God has an individual purpose for us to do. Unless we fulfill it, we are dissatisfied. We must embrace God's purposes. We cannot alter masculine and feminine simply by altering definitions to fit our cultural norms. We are fundamentally different than men in a world where distinctions between male and female have grown thin. But in a world of men, women are uniquely women!

How do women minister to women in the context of the local church? It starts when one woman looks for ways to share God's words of truth with another woman so that both will become fully developed Christ followers. And as these Christ followers connect with each other, the resulting fellowship and growth is powerful.

THINK IT OVER

1. Name one woman who has influenced your life for good.

2. What was the primary thing she did or said that caused you to personally grow as a woman?

3. What was the main thing she modeled in her life that influenced you to grow spiritually?

4. Name an experience you have had in which you depended on God. What comfort can you bring to someone from the Lord because of this?

5. How can you influence the women in your local church for good?

6. What would need to change for another woman in your local church to influence you for good?

7. What other example in the Bible shows how, because women understand each other, they influence each other for good?

THINK IT THROUGH

1. What are the areas in which you personally need to be understood?

2. What do you understand about women that would help the women in your church to mature as Christ followers?

3. Take the time to memorize and meditate on Ephesians 4:25–32. What five principles does Paul suggest will strengthen your understanding of relationships?
    a. Ephesians 4:25
    b. Ephesians 4:26
    c. Ephesians 4:29–30
    d. Ephesians 4:31
    e. Ephesians 4:32

Action Point: Take the time to write a thank-you note to the women in your life who have influenced you to live as a fully developed Christ follower.

NOTES

1. Faith Popcorn and Lys Marigold, *EVEolution: The Eight Truths of Marketing to Women* (New York: Hyperion, 2000), 7.
2. See Gary Chapman, *The Five Love Languages: How to Express Heartfelt Commitment to Your Mate* (Chicago: Moody, 1992).

WOMEN NEED WOMEN IN ORDER TO GROW

"Marriage relationships are wonderful, but even the best husband is deficient in meeting every relational need a woman has. My women friends fill in some of those deficiencies and for that I am glad!"

ROCHELLE BAUCOM

"Women need other women because they understand how to meet each other's social and spiritual needs. Women together are great! Godly women together spells growth!"

"For a woman, there is nothing better than the comfort of another woman's understanding and compassion. It doesn't change what's going on; it just reminds you that you can make it. Her ability to cry and laugh with you and at the same time remind you of her faithful God helps you grow up, even if just a little!"

"It has been said that to really know how to help someone move to another level of growth and understanding, one must walk in another's shoes. We women walk in each other's shoes a lot and know exactly what we mean without always saying everything there is to say!"

"In Joppa, there was a disciple named Tabitha [Dorcas] . . . she became sick and died . . . when he [Peter] arrived he was taken upstairs to the room. All the widows stood around him, crying and showing him the robes and other clothing that Dorcas had made while she was still with them."

Acts 9:36–37, 39

Chapter Seven

WOMEN NEED WOMEN
IN ORDER TO GROW

I first met Anne of Green Gables on my tenth birthday. For more than forty years, I have loved her spunk. I suspect many women share my feelings for this turn-of-the-last-century orphan girl. You may have seen the television version. To my way of thinking, it does not capture the wonderful descriptions by L. M. Montgomery of this pitiful but ingenious creature called Anne. The Anne series of books is the product of Montgomery's own childhood and great imagination. It is the story of how the aging siblings Marilla and Matthew Cuthbert mistakenly adopt Anne from a Prince Edward Island orphanage, thinking they are getting a boy to help them at Green Gables.

From the earliest pages of Anne Shirley's chatter to the closing chapters of her life as a grandmother, Anne captures the reader's heart. Only her imagination surpasses her creative use of the English language! Whether it is learning to get along with her foster mother, Marilla, adjusting to the sharp tongued and critical neighbor Mrs. Lynde, or being accepted by the girls who have been in Avonlea all their lives, Anne's story is not unlike that of many women I know. It is about how a little girl grows into a young woman, painfully aware of what it means to "fit in." Because of the girls and women in her life, Anne grows up to become a poised and gracious woman.

One of my favorite scenes includes the moments just before Anne meets Diana Barry, the girl who will be her friend. Your connections with women may not have the profound effect Anne's friendship does on her, but the words are a good reminder of the dynamic involved in women together. "Anne rose to her feet, with clasped hands, the tears still glistening on her cheeks. . . . 'Oh, Marilla, I'm frightened—now that it has come I'm actually frightened. What if she shouldn't like me! It would be the most tragical disappointment of my life.'"

Marilla urges her to stay unflustered and warns her not to use long words or give startling speeches, to be polite and well behaved. Anne, trembling, replies, "Oh, Marilla, you'd be excited, too, if you were going to meet a little girl you hoped to be your bosom friend and whose mother mightn't like you!"

When Anne meets Diana, from the depths of her heart she asks: "'Oh, Diana,' said Anne at last, clasping her hands and speaking almost in a whisper, 'do you think—oh, do you think you can like me a little—enough to be my bosom friend? . . . Will you swear to be my friend for ever and ever?'"

Diana, uncomfortable with the idea of "swearing" but assured by Anne it is not the wicked kind, agrees. "'We must join hands—so,' said Anne gravely. ' . . . I'll repeat the oath first. I solemnly swear to be faithful to my bosom friend, Diana Barry, as long as the sun and moon shall endure. Now you say it and put my name in.' Diana repeated the 'oath' with a laugh fore and aft." And so the friendship begins.

All of us at some time in our lives are like Anne Shirley and Diana Barry. We long for loyal friendship. We are eager to be liked by at least one other woman besides our mother. As we make connections with women, we discover that the giving and taking, the sharing of life together, helps to grow us up. As women who are Christ followers, we learn the wisdom of Proverbs 27:17, "As iron sharpens iron, so one man sharpens another" (quoheleth, "so a friend sharpens a friend").

As a ten-year-old, I began to hope for a "bosom friend," someone who would belong just to me. Over the years God has granted me friends like that. My first best friend came to Canada from Scotland when I was in junior high school. For five years we did everything together. Together we walked to school, ate lunch, attended church, talked on the phone, and double-dated. We did the hundreds of things girls love to do together. No one could break our friendship or separate our hearts. Even the smallest argument was like a sword to our souls. I recently found a box of old papers and discovered one from Maureen, a response to an apology I had made to her one day long ago. It is full of loving friendship, of humble confession, of loyalty and trust. Though after college we both married and I moved away, the bond remains. When we meet, it takes only seconds for us to return to our relationship of "kindred spirit." The added blessing in my life is that Maureen is a fervent follower of the Lord Jesus Christ. As girls from Christian homes with many imperfections, we helped each other grow in trust of the Savior.

In every city in which I've lived with a community of believers, God has given me more than "bosom friends." He gives godly sisters in Christ each step of the journey. And over the years it is only as I have mingled with women who love God more than I love Him that I have experienced the personal growth of maturity.

WOMEN TOGETHER—NOTHING NEW

You already know how natural it is for women to be together. We love to shop together, have lunch together, talk, laugh, walk, share concerns, and cry together. And when we are out for dinner, it's always more fun to go to the powder room together. Women spending time together isn't new. Women have done it since Eve gave birth to her first daughter who, if she married one of Eve's sons, became her daughter-in-law! (Don't forget, the gene pool in Adam and Eve's children was huge and had not been contaminated. A man could easily marry a sister without the problem of potential mutations.) But women's *coming together* doesn't need to be arranged. Serendipitous moments provide some of the best times together. Just recently at the supermarket where I shop, I saw the twenty-first century version of the ancient practice of women coming together. There, only steps inside the store, grouped in twos together, were about six women talking, laughing, wanting to mingle before they shopped because time with a friend can be among the favorite moments of many women's day.

The idea of women coming together just because we are women is not the focus of this book. Women around the world meet at the market, tell each other news of the day, and exchange ideas and personal plans. But once a woman becomes a serious Christ follower, she enters a world filled with sisters in Christ who offer potential for spiritual growth by virtue of mingling together. We recognize an amazing truth: Christian women are not created as clones of each other. Each one is placed by God in our lives in the context of our church or our community to bring us to a maturity impossible on our own. When godly women understand the greater purpose of spiritual growth in Christ, we witness a spiritual synergy that points to coming together for reasons greater than ourselves. The Bible gives us profound examples of good and bad ways of coming together.

The Hebrew Women Came Together

Take Miriam. Tambourine in hand to celebrate God's mighty deliverance from Egypt, Miriam leads the women, singing and dancing and saying: "Sing to the LORD, for he is highly exalted. The horse and its rider

he has hurled into the sea" (Exodus 15:21). Long before she draws the
women together for exuberant praise of Yahweh, she learns from her mother
to trust God even when life is hard. Do not miss the import of the female
connections in her life. We are not talking about someone who learns to
handle stress because the old house her mother bought has the wrong color
rug. We are not looking at a girl who is mature because she has attended a
charm school. We are meeting a young girl growing up under a foreign
and fierce government that cares little for the value of human life or the
ways of Yahweh.

As the daughter of Amram and Jochebed, Miriam knew what it was
to have parents who were slaves under Pharaoh (Exodus 2:1–9). As the
daughter of a godly mother, Miriam witnessed her mother's trust in God's
care for her family.

Miriam's nation had arrived in Egypt about four hundred years before
she was born because of the wisdom of Joseph who had been sold into slav-
ery by his brothers. Jacob arrived with his family in Egypt as the patriarch
of seventy members. In more than four hundred years, the twelve tribes
grew to two million people. Because of the Hebrew population explo-
sion, the Pharaoh who didn't know Joseph (Exodus 1:8) took drastic mea-
sures to protect his kingdom. Probably many Jewish male babies were killed.

Think of what Miriam learned in the presence of her mother and the
feisty midwives who feared Yahweh over the Egyptian king. She sees her
mother trust Yahweh when it is inconvenient to be pregnant. She is nearby as Jochebed gives birth to a beautiful boy (Hebrews 11:23), enabled by
midwives who feared God over Pharaoh, knowing Pharaoh was killing Jewish baby boys. She witnesses her parents' trust in Yahweh as Jochebed builds
the basket and sets it afloat in the Nile for Miriam to guard. She shares the
risk of faith, protecting her brother from the Egyptian crocodiles. She models wisdom and courage as she proposes to Pharaoh's daughter that her
mother care for Moses. She lives apart from her brother who lived in
Pharaoh's palace for forty years before he was chased out of Egypt for another forty years. She experiences the marvelous deliverance of Yahweh
from Egypt, led by her brother Moses. So when she realizes her options to
respond to God's deliverance, she does what godly women do: She draws
the Hebrew women together to offer praise.

One caution as we learn lessons from Miriam: She faces the temptation all who serve together will someday face. Jealousy. Envy. Greed. The
Spirit of God through Moses puts her name ahead of Aaron's in the story

of their grumbling about the Cushite wife Moses had chosen (Numbers 12:1–9). It must have been her idea to gossip about Moses' leadership.

Let it be said that every criticism of the heart reaches the ear of God. The words we speak against a sister or a brother do not go unnoticed by the Lord. If you read on in Numbers 12, you will see what the Lord does about the critical spirit of Miriam and Aaron. He summons the siblings, including Moses, to the Tent of Meeting and warns Miriam and Aaron about speaking against Moses. It is Yahweh who establishes Moses' right to lead; Miriam and Aaron do not. And when a person causes disunity and speaks against His choice, he or she is meddling where one should never meddle. The startling thing is this: When the cloud is lifted and the Lord's presence leaves them, Miriam stands alone and leprous. She is kept outside the camp for seven days. Her sin keeps the people from moving on. After seven days, in answer to Aaron's cry and Moses' prayer, Miriam is brought back into the fellowship of the nation (Numbers 12:10–16). I have often fallen on my knees in the presence of God, aware of my own critical heart, and thanked Him that He does not strike me with leprosy when I am careless in my thoughts or words about God's leaders. Perhaps if He did, our churches would be spiritually healthier, better able to know unity.

The warning to us is this: None of us is ever beyond the temptation to spoil the Spirit's ministry in the world through our church. Our very penchant for coming together in unity and joy has the potential for spiritual disaster in our local churches when we refuse to submit to God's Spirit. The cults of our day and pagans around us will not threaten our unity; a critical spirit among sisters in Christ will.

New Testament Women Struggled with Unity

In the New Testament, there is an interesting relationship worth noticing because of its implication for the church today. It is found in Philippians 4:2–3 and concerns two women who at one time were probably "bosom friends." They were clearly at the heart of what went on in the Philippian church. It is hard to know what place women played in the Philippian church except to say it was an important one. Finding no synagogue in Philippi, for lack of ten Jewish men, Paul went down to the river, expecting to find a place of prayer. He found women gathered together for prayer, including Lydia, a God-fearer. Acts 16:13–15 indicates that Lydia and her household believed the gospel, were baptized, and immediately welcomed the church to meet in her home. What follows is typical for Paul. He was beaten, jailed for preaching in Philippi, and then escorted out of the city. When Paul writes a letter back to the Philippian church, he urges them repeatedly to "stand firm in the unity of the gospel" as though disunity was a problem. Paul's purpose statement for his letter could be summarized by Philippians 1:27–28a: "Whatever happens, conduct yourselves in a manner worthy of the gospel of Christ. Then, whether I come and see you or only hear about you in my absence, I will know that you stand firm in one spirit, contending as one man for the faith of the gospel without being frightened in any way by those who oppose you."

It also indicates that his plea to the women in Philippians 4:2–3 is warranted. He calls on the whole church to stand firm in the Lord, pleading emotionally with Euodia and Syntyche to agree with each other in the Lord. He asks the "loyal yokefellow" to help these two to get along, since they were once contenders with Paul for the gospel.

Few commentators speculate as to the problem between these women, Euodia and Syntyche. There is nothing in the text to identify the source of their grievance. From the flavor of the letter, there is plenty of reason to believe it has to do with a broken relationship. Based on the teaching of this book, it could be a difference of opinion on anything from how to present the gospel to being fearful of or in disagreement about those who oppose them, from selfishness (Philippians 2:1–4) to a misunderstanding of true humility as modeled by Jesus Christ (vv. 5–11) or complaining about serving in the local church (vv. 14–18). It might be a disagreement on who was the best if one is putting confidence in the flesh (3:2–10), or it could be a stressful situation caused by those who are enemies of the Cross (vv. 17–21).

Whether they were deaconesses or wives of leaders, we don't know. We know they were distinguished ladies of the church and were not getting along.[1] We don't know how they publicly treated each other, but we do know their bickering was a concern to Paul. He was grieved not simply because of their broken friendship but because their fighting and refusal to get along threatened the unity of the Philippian church. They were not obeying the appeal to "stand fast in the Lord." The command to get along must be applied at the individual level if it is to work among the entire church. Paul's appeal to these women to "be of the same mind in the Lord" was public. I have often thought how politically incorrect the Bible is in serious cases of sin. The Holy Spirit mentions names and events without embarrassment, all so we can learn the importance of living together in harmony. Paul said that if these women will not voluntarily come together and forgive each other, the assistance of the unidentified "loyal yokefellow" will be required.

This broken friendship required a third person to mediate this relationship that was causing disunity in the local church.

So, What Should Women Do?

Some women will never choose to be with women in an organized fashion. They don't care for women. An overseas pastor's wife wrote this note to me following a workshop I taught urging women to see how the local church is enriched when women come joyfully together. She answers the question I ask whenever I speak to women: "Why should women minister to women?"

> *We understand each other! I often minister to other women, but to be completely honest, I don't like women! I don't particularly like women's meetings either! I am a pastor's wife and I do it because it is expected of me. Sometimes I wish that I could enjoy it but I have this mental block where I don't want to be typecast, and yet when I watch and listen to what you are saying, I would like to change! There! Has that confused you? Because I'm still in a muddle as to what I should do for women and what is expected of me!*

There is no time in this book to address the particular concern of my friend, the pastor's wife. But I can say that some women prefer a male world. If they are married, they like to be with their husbands, couples, or the women married to their husband's best friends. If they are single, they may be content with one or two close girlfriends but mostly interact in a male world. But based on the genetic code and the witness of Scripture, there is clear evidence that when women come together for purposes of edifying each other and not just their own comfort, they sharpen each other and grow toward maturity. They leave behind the actions of little girls where high control is the order of the day and learn to adopt the holy charm and godly poise that Peter describes in his letter to the churches (1 Peter 3:5).

If you are a woman who is a Christ follower and a leader in women's ministries, look around your church. What kind of women do you want to grow? Independent women who are isolated islands, creating their own worlds and focused on their own needs? Or do you want to begin with the end in mind? The purposes of God through the rich resources of women in your church include growing women who model a faith in hard times like Jochebed. They help other women lift high the name of the Lord without drawing attention to themselves. God's purposes include

godly women in the local church who willingly obey His Word and repeatedly and regularly forgive. They refuse to behave in histrionic and self-
centered ways. Instead these women help each other grow from girlhood
to godly womanhood. They put away their differences and see the chance
for Christian friendship as the means whereby Christ glues the church
they are in together. And the promise is that the whole world watches and
gives glory to God.

Think Link

Faith Popcorn, in *EVEolution,* suggests that no one serious about marketing for women ignores the fact that women love to be together. And
the way women are made, according to Popcorn is this:"Think Link. Don't
think pink!"[2]

How is the spiritual health of your church? How is your own spiritual
health? What kind of "bosom friends" are you cultivating? If being a woman
means anything, it means being the godly woman your church needs so that
unity will prevail. Miriam and Euodia and Syntyche teach us the value of
personal holiness as it fits into the unity of the church. Regardless of your
personality, age, stage, or gifts, realize the important part godly women in
your local church play in your life. Based on the foundation we have laid
that the church is the natural birthing room where babies are born and children are cared for, look for women who model what you want to learn.
No one woman will teach you everything. But every woman in your local
church, regardless of your likes or differences, can teach you something. In
fact, I believe it is impossible for any woman to grow to maturity apart from
healthy female relationships in the body of Christ.

Determine to Build Not Tear Down Relationships

When our children became teenagers, we urged them to plan ahead
how they would behave in certain circumstances. Wisdom always determines what it will do before the choice needs to be made. In the back of
the car there is no time to decide in the same way there is when you are
at home, considering how to behave. The same is true with growing friendships. Determine that the women in your church are there so you can
grow together, maturing in ways you could never do alone as you learn to
share and get along with other family members.

In the next chapter, I will suggest ten building blocks for you to begin to use as the basis on which to grow together in your friendships with women. For now, let me suggest some practical guidelines that will help you build relationships with the women in your local church. They are links that build relationships and come from a book my husband wrote a number of years ago called *Quality Friendship.* Gary offers biblical principles for connecting well with others.

Grow Your Friendships

Using the close friendship of David and Jonathan as his model, Gary offers five decisions a good friend will need to make in order for relationships to grow. But you will need to determine these things as you mingle with women in your church.

Model an Attitude of Acceptance. As you begin to grow as a Christ follower, you may be tempted to evaluate women on the same basis as the world does. "Is she my kind of woman? Does she like the same things? Does she know the right people?" Even a leader in women's ministries will have her own special friends, but nowhere in the New Testament are believers allowed to create cliques. Paul says in 1 Corinthians 1:10–17 that a party spirit is evidence of worldliness not spirituality. For your women's ministries to thrive, you will need to decide that you will cultivate an attitude of acceptance toward each woman God has placed in your local church. The practical ramifications of this choice are enormous. It means there are no divisions big enough to separate women from each other. When this attitude is absent, the potential for division and disunity is huge. Only the Holy Spirit of God can place in your heart the attitude of acceptance regardless of all the human things you would allow to keep women apart.

Recognize the Factor of Mutual Attraction. Although it is important to cultivate acceptance, there will be times when God puts in your life an Anne Shirley or a Diana Barry. There are going to be women whose heart beats with yours and whose personality complements yours. Just reading through the letters of Paul tells you he had some men with whom he enjoyed a great camaraderie (Luke, Timothy, Silas, Barnabas). They served together because they liked each other. Don't be afraid to partner with those whose temperament fits yours. Even with close friendships, as you grow together, be sure your focus is God so your relationship stays healthy and others are not made to feel excluded.

Express Your Commitment. God has expressed His commitment to us in hundreds of ways in His Word. He has told us He loves us, will finish what He has started, and will never leave us or forsake us. David and Jonathan entered into a verbal covenant to express their commitment to each other, not unlike the one David's great-grandmother Ruth gave to her mother-in-law, Naomi, in Ruth 1:16–18. Committing your loyalty as a friend may be difficult to do. But it is a necessity in order for the relationship to grow. Gary says:

> *It has been my observation that in our society, women are more skilled at forming deep relationships than men. . . . Perhaps it is at the point of verbalizing our commitment that we need to do some hard thinking about the quality of our friendships. I have found that as I speak more openly about my commitment to a friend, I am able to give of myself more freely.[3]*

Adopt Genuine Openness. A fourth link in building relationships is transparency, authenticity, the quality that makes friendships grow. When we hide from each other or spend our lives criticizing each other, we end up with no ability to have a relationship. For many years, I had a friend whom I really never knew; when I moved to another place, I realized she really never knew who I was either. She could never speak openly of her weaknesses or her strengths. Genuine openness does not tell all, but it tells enough so the person whose life you are building into can see who you are and what you desire to become. As long as you live in the shadows, you will have something to hide. When you walk in the light, you can live with genuine openness before the women in your church, who will appreciate meeting someone truly authentic and sincere.

Appreciate Mutual Enjoyment. There is nothing quite so wonderful as being able to be yourself with another sister in Christ. There is joy and safety in appreciating your friends for who they are and, as Peter would say, in letting "love cover a multitude of sins." Gary's words are worth quoting here as we identify this last building block. He says:

> *Some people have difficulty developing friendships just because they are so intense about their friends that they literally smother friendship. They see every moment of weakness on the part of a friend—bad humor, moodiness—as a sign that the friendship is in trouble. They are very sensitive to imagined slights and are easily offended. As a result, they always seem to be watching their friends, and one can never relax and enjoy*

being a friend. Friendship involves a confidence in the other person that is very giving, but also undemanding. Friendship is to be enjoyed, not endlessly analyzed. [4]

Women need women in order to grow. And whether you are committed to a bosom friend or a group of women in your local church, you will need to determine what kind of building blocks you are going to use in order to link up with other women for their good, your own good, and the glory of God.

THINK IT OVER

1. Who in your life has been a "kindred spirit" as you have walked with the Lord? What has she taught you about godly living?

2. What do you consider to be the best circumstances for women to grow together?

3. What woman have you observed in your local church who has healthy relational qualities you desire? What are you willing to do to spend time with her so you can grow in these areas?

4. Of the "five ways to build a relationship," which do you do best? What in your life proves that?

5. Examine your personal relationships. What would you need to change to more successfully practice the "five ways to build a relationship" with your friends?

THINK IT THROUGH

Take some time to evaluate some of the friendship partners in God's Word. Some examples of these would be

• Ruth and Naomi	Ruth 1:6–19
• David and Jonathan	1 Samuel 20
• Isaiah and Hezekiah	2 Chronicles 32:20–23
• Jehoiada and Joash	2 Chronicles 24:1–3, 8–13, 17–22
• Euodia and Syntyche	Philippians 4:2–3

- Paul and Silas   Acts 16:16–40
- Paul and Luke   Colossians 4:14; 2 Timothy 4:9–13
- Paul and Timothy   2 Timothy 1:3–14

NOTES

1. F. F. Bruce, gen. ed., *The International Bible Commentary* (Grand Rapids: Eerdmans, 1965), 1041.
2. Faith Popcorn and Lys Marigold, *EVEolution: The Eight Truths of Marketing to Women* (New York: Hyperion, 2000), 9.
3. Gary Inrig, *Quality Friendship* (Chicago: Moody, 1981), 56.
4. Ibid., 57–58.

Chapter Eight

BUILDING HEALTHY
RELATIONSHIPS

"One woman can relate to another woman only as far as she herself has gone with God. The unique emotions of a woman are understood by God because He has made us. As we are comforted by Him, so we can turn around and relate to others."

"The wise woman builds her house, but with her own hands the foolish one tears hers down."

Proverbs 14:1

Chapter Eight

BUILDING HEALTHY RELATIONSHIPS

*Y*ou may have a friend like Anne Shirley or Diana Barry, or you may be without a "kindred spirit." If you have one, she may be your sister by birth or your sister in the Lord. The truth of the times in which we live is this: In spite of the technology that lets us communicate more efficiently, many women admit to living in an emotional and relational wasteland. For women, wired for relationships, that can be the loneliest state in the world. It is also the reason women who care about the emotional and spiritual health of women in their churches initiate ways to bring women together in a godly atmosphere. But understand this: Any social club can bring women together. For a local church to provide a healthy coming together requires godly leadership to begin with the end in mind. What initiatives will protect the personal and corporate spiritual growth of women in this local church? What building blocks will the church need to provide so it remains a healthy organism offering a safe place for women to grow and mature?

BUILDING A SAFE PLACE TOGETHER

The primary function of women in a healthy women's ministry is to help us come into the presence of God, and that can only happen if we offer relational safety to each other. It is the very thing that is missing for women today. There may be no spiritual or relational safety in their homes, their neighborhoods, their places of employment. So when women come into the ministries provided by the local church, it is essential that they know it to be a safe place. What does it mean for women to offer other women a safe place in the context of the local church? I believe it means this: When you attend a Bible study, prayer group, mother's club, outreach tea/coffee, or discipleship class, we will treat you with great value. We will not speak to you disparagingly or discuss you when you leave the room. When we invite you to an outreach event, a retreat, or a leadership meeting,

we will do our best to let you know that the core values God has set forth
in His Word are the values that determine our behavior. We will do everything we can to reflect His character in all our behaviors.

To ensure this functions from the inside out, the Women's Leadership
Core in our local church Women's Ministry has agreed on CORE values
that reflect the greater values of our church. We have developed a mission
statement that determines how the values are put to work for women.
(See Appendix.) Women in leadership at every level sign a covenant committing to certain principles that intentionally produce "safe places." As a
daily practice with volunteers and paid staff, attendees and participants, we
encourage the concept of building up rather than tearing down. Does that
mean everyone who comes to Trinity Women's Ministries *feels* safe? We
pray they all do. But without a doubt, we do all we can for them to *know*
they are in a safe place.

Principles for Building

In order to create a safe place for women to come, we have committed
to practice practical holiness. At the heart of women growing together is
the fact that how we relate is all about how much we resemble the Lord
Jesus Christ. When you stop expecting others to be what you are not and
become a reflection of who God is to those in your life, you will find yourself building healthy relationships and not tearing them down.

The Wise Woman Builds

The basis for any healthy relationship between women is given to us
in God's Word. Relationship begins with God, the Three in One, who enjoys perfect harmony in relationship as Father, Son, and Holy Spirit. When
God created Adam and Eve, He enjoyed an intimate, sacred relationship
with them. They in turn enjoyed intimacy with each other. But sin changed
their relationship with God and each other. The healthy relationship was
torn down, never to be the same again. It is only as we become new creatures in Christ Jesus empowered by the Holy Spirit that any of us can begin to build healthy relationships with others that last a lifetime.

Both Old and New Testaments record holiness as a command for those
who profess to have God's life within them. It is given three times in Leviticus 11:44–45; 19:2; and 20:7 as the way the nation of Israel is to conduct
itself. It is repeated in 1 Peter 1:15–16, where Peter says:"But just as he who

called you is holy, so be holy in all you do; for it is written: 'Be holy, because I am holy.'"

Like many commands in Scripture, we are called to be holy because it
matches the behavior and character of the God we serve. To be holy means
to be set apart for God's use or purpose. It means to conform to God's
purpose for your life. When a chair is sat upon, that chair is achieving the
purpose for which it has been set apart. If I see you walking around with
the chair dangling over your shoulder, I will ask you, "What are you doing
with that chair? You missed the point of its purpose! It was made to be sat
upon, not to hang around your neck!"

So it is with believers. As women indwelt by the Holy Spirit, we are
made for a relationship with God so we can turn around and reflect His
character. We function best when we fulfill the purpose for which God
has chosen us: to be holy as He is holy. As women, wired for relationships,
our mandate is to reflect the character of our holy God to each other. As with
other commands, God graciously gives us the reason He commands us to
be holy in all we do: It is to reflect the character of the One to whom we
belong. The measure of building healthy relationships is not so much finding ourselves as it is finding our Master. When we find our Master—the triune, holy God—we find our purpose for living.

The perfect model of relationships, the Lord Jesus Christ as God come
in the flesh, reveals God to us. As our Savior, He modeled healthy relationships within the Trinity: He does the will of the Father. He modeled
healthy relationships with His family, though they did not believe in Him.
He built healthy relationships with His followers, men of very different per-
sonalities. As we come into His family, we discover that He is our model
of how we treat each other.

Building Blocks for Relationships

Our ministry has developed ten building blocks for effective ministry
between women. These are things every woman can use as building blocks
for solid relationships with the women in her life. When you give away what
God has given you, you are able to offer women a safe place where relationships can flourish. I urge you to do this: Plan to give away these qualities in your relationships with women instead of demanding them. In the
end, you will personally become the faithful friend that Timothy was to
Paul and that women in your church need. Your ministry will become the

safe place women need. Together, you will become women of worth with whom other women feel safe because you have embraced the heart of God.

The following is not an exhaustive list of relational building blocks. But they are essential if women are going to get along together. They are necessary in order to build healthy relationships among women in the local church. They are primary if a group of women want to provide a safe place for women to be. As you consider them, recognize they are the way God relates to His children. They are the gifts He gives that enables each one of us to find in Him a safe place, a secure relationship that flourishes into a bosom friend.

Security: You Are Safe with Me; You Belong. God provides security to believers through the death of His Son, Jesus Christ. We are saved from our sin and ourselves. God gives us eternal life, and we have the confidence of being loved and belonging to Him. When women come to seek friendship in the context of women's ministries, they need to know they have come to a group of women whose confidence is not in their clothing or performance but in Someone grander than themselves. When you find your security in Christ alone, you are able to forget yourself and concentrate on making others feel welcome and safe. You model the message "You belong here" regardless of social status or ethnic or denominational differences.

Significance: "You Matter" Although You Are Different from Me. In God's scheme of things, different is good; harmony is desirable. Anyone who enjoys an orchestra knows the beauty of the evening is not in hearing only the lead violin but in listening to the combination of different sounds. Paul told us all believers are significant and warned against a party spirit that values one and not the other (1 Corinthians 1:10–13). True harmony in relationships comes when we rejoice in the particular way God has gifted us and when we complete the one who is different from us. Don't compete with each other. Commit to celebrate the differences and tell each woman "you matter."

Grace: I Will Give You the Opposite of What You Deserve. No one who understands the grace of God in her life will treat others ungraciously. God's grace gives us the opposite of what we deserve. We deserve hell; He gives us heaven. We deserve to pay for our sin; He pays for them Himself and gives us salvation. He blesses us every morning with His faithfulness (Lamentations 3:23). Grace allows God to accept us even when we are a mess (Ephesians 2:1–8). It requires Him to transform us. His acceptance of us is not so much unconditional—that may never motivate change—as it is gracious. Grace means He has a preferred future for us. He sees the big picture of what we are supposed to be. Healthy relationships among women are won or lost on the issue of grace. Withholding grace from a sister in Christ goes against God's gift to you. If you know a truly gracious person, you know she is the best antidote to pride and arrogance, to fear and anxiety. She gives away grace; she offers loyal kindness. She, strongly humble, comes to the aid of the weak and fearful and doesn't demand perfection. She does for them what they can't do for themselves.

Encouragement: I Will Support and Protect You. The Bible is full of God speaking words of encouragement to His children. More than three hundred times throughout Scripture, He says, "Do not be afraid!" He has supported and encouraged and protected His children for centuries. That is just how He is! Whether it is to Hagar in a desert place (Genesis 21:17–21), to King Jehoshaphat in 2 Chronicles 20:15, to the apostle Paul in Acts 18:9–11, or to hundreds of His children in between, He says, "Do not be afraid!" You model God in your relationships not when you criticize and tear down your leaders or pass judgment on others who do not agree with your opinions. You model God most when you come alongside and support, encourage, and verbally protect those who are your friends. If the eyes of the Lord range throughout the earth to strengthen those whose hearts are fully committed to Him (2 Chronicles 16:9), how can women in the local church meet His approval? In your arsenal of tools for providing a safe place, encouragement and verbal support build others up.

Forgiveness: The Offended Party Pays. At the heart of the gospel is the forgiveness of sins. John says in 1 John 1:9, "If we confess our sins, he is faithful and just and will forgive us our sins and purify us from all unrighteousness [that which escapes our scrutiny]." Only God can forgive our sins, because we have sinned against Him. The Lord Jesus taught Peter that it isn't a matter of keeping records on how many times you have been forgiven (Matthew 18:21–22). The greatest relationship builder is the woman who lives a repenting lifestyle before God and models a forgiving spirit to those within the body of believers. Forgiveness says, "I will pay the price" but does not excuse the sin. Although forgiveness is always possible, reconciliation may not be. The teaching of Ephesians 4:25–32 makes possible safe relationships because we are forgivers.

Honesty: I Make the Commitment to Live Congruently and Transparently.
God models honesty before creation and in His church. When He speaks,
He tells the truth. He does not lie. No one in the universe will ever be
able to say He has not spoken clearly about His power and divine nature
(Romans 1:18–20). Anyone who takes the time to read Scripture will dis-
tinctly hear the Father's heart. Any who wish to know His heart can see
the Savior model congruency in private and public life. The One who has
called us to be holy in all we do calls us to transparent, authentic relationships with each other. That does not mean "freedom of speech." It does
not mean telling everyone what is in your mind. It does mean "freedom
to speak wholesome words" as Paul teaches in Ephesians 4:29. When you
live consistently and speak the truth in love, Proverbs says your speech is like
apples of gold in settings of silver (Proverbs 25:11). Women find safety
with women whose words are fitly spoken.

Respect: I Value Your Worth. For many years I was led to believe that
"just loving" people was the key to healthy relationships. The problem with
that advice is I didn't know what I was supposed to feel. The love for someone I was struggling with eluded me. Then I realized that there is a pre-
requisite to loving someone. It is having regard for the person's worth
regardless of his or her behaviors. Respect is giving the gift of worth. It is
the attitude God has toward us as He works to win and woo us through
the work of His Holy Spirit. It is not because our behavior is good but
because we are the product of His creative hand, made in His own image,
that He values our worth.

If you have come to understand how much the Father values you, you
will understand a little of why He sent His beloved Son to die for you on
the cross. He did not die for animals or angels but for Adam's race. That is
an act of love before any transformation takes place. The women in your
life do not need you to change them. The women in your local church
and the friends you are seeking to influence need your respect. They need
to know you value them as women with potential for great impact on
others. Before you can show them you love them, they need your vote of
respect. Three by-products of this attitude are obvious. First, the fear of
the Lord is the beginning of wisdom. That means I understand that the
highest value in the universe is not the life of man. It is the personhood of
God. He alone deserves the highest regard, the most high place of honor.
Only those who hold the God of heaven in high regard can model the attitude of respecting others. Second, it is only when you respect God ap-

propriately that you gain a healthy self-respect. Self-respect is not a product of your own doing. It means you accept God's evaluation of the value of your life. It means you understand that apart from Him, there is no value to your life, just as without the signature of Leonardo da Vinci, the *Mona Lisa* is valueless. Third, holding God in high regard, valuing human life as second in worth only to God means you will have a healthy respect for others, from the unborn human to the aged. No one, regardless of age or stage, is worthless, though we are unworthy to be called His children and heirs with His Son. When you give away "respect" and "high regard" you provide the safe place women need in order to be loved and to grow.

In *Bound by Honor,* Gary Smalley says: "Honor is a decision we make to place high value, worth and importance on another person by viewing him or her as a priceless gift and granting him or her a position in our lives worthy of great respect."[1]

Love: I Choose to Meet the Need. In Leviticus 19:18 where God commands His people to love their neighbors as themselves, He does so in the context of people being tempted to hold a grudge. Jesus repeats the command in Luke 10:27 when He answers a scribe who is questioning Him. The word for love in this case is *agape.* It focuses on the need of the person to be loved rather than the need of the person who is to love. The answer precedes the parable of the Good Samaritan where Jesus says the love that chooses to meet the need can be seen more than felt (Luke 10:29–37). Who is your neighbor? It is the woman (or man or child) whose need you can meet, beginning with those in your family and your church and moving into the community and beyond. Love is the motivation that keeps us from staying in our comfort zones or just having coffee with the girls at the church. Love is the factor that compels us to reach out to women whose lives are empty, whose relationships are broken. Love is the gift God has given us that we cannot ignore as we minister to women around us. Paul explains why in 2 Corinthians 5:14: "Christ's love compels us." The King James Version does not say "love *for* Christ constraineth us," though that surely is true if we know the Savior intimately. It says "the love *of* Christ" constrains us. Paul follows that statement with two important statements. First, he says the effect of Christ's love in dying on the cross is so that we will no longer live for ourselves but for Him. Second, he says this kind of love transforms the way we see people: "So from now on we regard no one from a worldly point of view" (2 Corinthians 5:16).

Paul's discussion focuses on the ministry of reconciliation we have with people because of God's love for us. It is love of Christ that propels us to implore and appeal to others to become a friend of God. Love has the potential for transforming your cozy Christian group into an outreaching community of Good Samaritans, ambassadors who appeal to women to be reconciled to God and one another. Love puts decisions we make toward others into action.

Discipline: I Take Responsibility. There is a lot of talk these days about spiritual disciplines, holy habits, and solitude. Experiences from Christ's life are used to illustrate how He went up into the mountain to pray to His Father. As women in a hurried culture, there will never be enough time to do everything we want to do. But as those who belong to Christ, we will have all the time we need to do the will of God. Jesus Himself said: "For I have come down from heaven not to do my will but to do the will of him who sent me" (John 6:38). Paul at the end of his life assured Timothy in 2 Timothy 4:6–7 that "the time has come for my departure. I have fought the good fight, I have finished the race, I have kept the faith." The only way a Christ follower can finish well is if she takes responsibility to work out her salvation with fear and trembling. We do not become models worth imitating or mentors who influence others for good with a program or impressive event. We affect others for their good and the glory of God by maintaining a holy lifestyle. We develop holy habits in the rhythm of everyday life that make it possible to listen to God's Word, to respond to His Holy Spirit, and to take up the cross daily and follow the Lord Jesus.

The idea of discipline is "to place in the mind." To ignore the intentional practice of godly disciplines, according to Paul in Romans 12:1–2, is to allow yourself to be shaped by the culture around you, letting the world squeeze you into its own mold (Phillips translation). When you offer yourself daily, for whatever length of time you choose to set aside, you are putting yourself in the place of solitude where the Holy Spirit through God's Word can begin to remold your mind from within. When that happens, you will desire to practice the will of God whose plan for you is good and acceptable and allows you to grow up. You and I can only place in another woman's mind what God has first taught us. You cannot teach what you do not know. You do not know what you do not practice. So discipline is a matter of the heart. It is a matter of the will. It is shaped for us the same way it was shaped for all saints before us: in the middle of living, in the center of relationships.

The women with whom you come in contact will know whether you have developed godly habits. They will know by the way you use your tongue, by the way you spend your money, by the things you do with your discretionary time. Discipline is like that. It is not hiding away in silence so much as it is a daily, weekly, monthly, yearly taking stock of your mind and graciously but firmly practicing the will of God. When you discipline yourself, you are able to place healthy habits in the minds of your friends.

Knowledge of God: The Great Indispensable. The last building block is not last because it is least important. It is the foundation on which every healthy relationship rests. It is the primary and essential relationship. It is impossible for anyone to be holy apart from a personal relationship with the Holy God who has come in human flesh to pay for the sins of those who believe in Him. If you desire to build healthy relationships, you will need to get to know God. To get to know God in the way He has clearly revealed Himself is to get to know His Word. I cannot say this enough. In fact, I would like to say it using the words of Leonard Sweet in a penetrating book he has written for this generation. He says we are "in a culture of Bible-believing churches filled with people who don't read the Bible . . . in a culture of soul-saving churches filled with people who never get personally involved with soul-saving."[2]

The greatest gift you can give any human being is a passion for God's Word. When you communicate the all-sufficient Word as the food, the water, the honey, the gold, the treasure that women need, you are fulfilling God's purposes for you as you serve women in the local church. It is not enough to have a surface handle on Scripture. It is essential to be able to "handle the Word" and to be able to "teach what is good" so you will have the eternal resource you need to answer the questions of women in your life, to give hope to women of your generation.

In 1966 to 1969, I sat in a classroom at Dallas Seminary and learned the wonders of God's Word, how to study it, why to study it, and the differences it would make in my life when I received and obeyed it. In 1970, a few months after we had had our second child, our son Stephen, I fell into a deep postnatal depression. The satisfying nature of God's Word eluded me. The pressures of real life stole away the thirst-quenching effect of the Word created in me by the Holy Spirit. God's Word was dry and tasteless to me. In a day when counselors were not as available as they are now, my husband walked me through this time. Battling my suicidal and negative thoughts, he made a comment that gave me hope. He said, "Only those who know God have the right to think positively because God is true and His words are truth." With that wise counsel and more sleep, I began to read the

Psalms even though I didn't want to. I began to listen to David who at times was running for his very life. His despair enabled me to begin to understand that in the deepest trials of life, there is hope for the one who has come to know God. This hope is written down in sixty-six marvelous books.

I can't tell you how long it took me to come back to a normal equilibrium. I don't remember. Sometimes women ask me, "Was your depression emotional, spiritual, physical, hormonal?" I don't really know. It was probably all of the above. But I do know this: As a young mother trying to care for two babies under fourteen months, I was believing lies about the value of my life and those of my children. Only as I sat quietly in my little house in Winnipeg on a cold winter day and read the eternal, thirst-quenching, life-giving words of the triune God did my soul begin to soften. And the Holy Spirit began to reawaken the hunger of my heart for Him. The God of the Bible is the indispensable relationship for every woman you will ever serve or serve with. There is no substitute. We in this culture are good at substitutes. We will do anything—plan fancy programs, busy ourselves with secondary things, keep our minds focused on any other book—we will do anything but stop to study God's Word so we can get to know God's person. Ultimately, all our plans for the greatest strategies in the world will fail if we do not introduce women to the one true God. Every program we micromanage is irrelevant if it does not help women move closer to the Lord Jesus Christ.

The God of the Bible has provided what we need for life and godliness. He has given us all the resources we will ever need to bring women to know Him. Our responsibility is to model what God has revealed to us and demonstrated for us.

CONCLUSION

These ten building blocks for building healthy relationships will serve as a model of personal growth. As you give away these qualities to others, you will provide the safe place they need. The bridges you build toward them will allow them to know the growth and safety in relationships that is a reflection of the holy God Himself.

THINK IT OVER

Anyone who builds a structure knows that the materials you use matter. You cannot use weak and flimsy material if you are building a sturdy bridge. You

also cannot be careless in the materials you use when you are building relationships in the family of God or with those you are seeking to reach for
Him. You will need these building blocks to build healthy relationships that
keep the unity in the body of Christ.

1. Describe what a holy person looks like. Have you ever met one? What
   characteristics are most noticeable about him or her?

2. Which of the ten building blocks can be said to be generally true of
   you? How do you demonstrate them?

3. Which of the ten building blocks do you wish to see the Holy Spirit
   develop in your life? How will you demonstrate them?

4. Describe God as you have come to know Him through the Lord Jesus.

5. To whom have you introduced the Lord Jesus recently? How do you
   make sure you are witnessing for the Lord Jesus in all your relationships?

THINK IT THROUGH

Women's ministries live or die on the basis of healthy relationships. During the following days, read the book of Proverbs. There are thirty-one
chapters, one for each day in the month. As you read through it, jot down
all the instructions the authors give as to how to live wisely. You will be surprised at how the fear of God and wisdom in relationships are connected.
Be holy because He who calls you is holy.

NOTES

1. Gary and Greg Smalley, *Bound by Honor* (Wheaton, Ill.: Tyndale, 1998), 14.
2. Leonard Sweet, *Postmodern Pilgrims* (Nashville: Broadman & Holman, 2000), iii.

Chapter Nine

WOMEN ARE NATURAL NURTURERS

"We women not only need to share and be empathetic to other women; we are wired by God to receive the nurturing women give that complements the care men give to women."

❧

"Women share common traits, desires, lifestyles, roles in life and therefore can relate and identify with each other. Shared experiences and feelings can provide a strong base for potential spiritual growth. Women are probably more comfortable being open with other women (generally speaking) than with men about many subjects."

❧

"I believe women should nurture women because they are more able to encourage, convict, challenge, listen, relate—all caregiving actions—in a way that gives us a living example of what to model. When I'm wondering what to do about something, I call one of my mentors and feel so refreshed because she understands what I am talking about. She gives me something specifically from God's Word to work on."

❧

"Women, single or married, enjoy encouraging each other, sharing their likes and dislikes. Just to have a friend and just to talk!"

ALBERTA HANSON, Hostess and Greeter, Women's Ministries

❧

"My mother taught me life skills but she did not know how to emote. I didn't wonder that she didn't love me. I just couldn't feel her love. When I began to come to Bible study and met women who could touch my arm gently or hug me to show they cared, I was blown away. And it wasn't just one woman who nurtured me. It was many and in so many lovely ways. I didn't know being nurtured felt that good! I am learning how to be a nurturer to other women."

Chapter Nine

WOMEN ARE NATURAL NURTURERS

*O*ne of the most fascinating birds I have watched recently is the plover—
a long-legged, loud screeching bird the size of a magpie. I first met
the black-and-white plover on a conference ground on Phillip Island, an island in the southern part of Australia. As I walked toward the mobile home
where I would spend the weekend, the baby plovers were walking in the
dew-drenched grass, skittering nervously away from my steps. Coming toward me with a vengeance was the mother plover.

"Don't go any closer to the chicks or the mother plover will swoop at
you and peck your eyes out!" the young custodian of the grounds warned
me. He had been swooped at one too many times by the protective mother.
The idea that she would poke her needle-like beak anywhere near my
eyes was enough to quicken my step! Out of the corner of my eye, I could
see another plover. It was the father who stood guard as the mother chased
the three little ones away from me.

Over the weekend I became captivated with the habits of this bird family. Since they were firmly entrenched on the grass outside the home, I knew
I would need to use my best manners as I tramped across the grass to the
dining room and chapel. In the early mornings, the mother sat round and
alert, huddling the chicks under her wings. During the day, when the babies were running around in their newfound freedom, she never let them
out of her sight. Always watching, she spent her day seeking food and caring for her young. The father plover stood at a distance, attentive and ready
to spring into action should anyone mess with the wife and babies.

I tried constantly to get close-ups of the plover family at play and being fed. The day I came very close to one of the babies, a most interesting
thing happened. Faced with an alien creature and imminent danger, the baby
plover instinctively pulled its skinny legs under its body and lay flat on the
ground as though dead, waiting to be rescued by its mother. My camera
clicked on this downy lump with nervous flickering eyes. I could hear the

hostile squawking of the mother plover moving closer to rescue her baby and threaten my safety. I didn't wait to see what plover mothers do to people who come too close to their babies. I already knew the mother was committed to caring for her young.

Plovers are not the only ones in God's creation to be prepared to take care of younger members of the species. I am convinced that what God has built into His physical creation teaches us a lot about spiritual caregiving. It is no mistake that women are physically shaped to nurture and nourish young babies. As maturing Christ followers, we are spiritually shaped to take care of the women God has put in our lives. By the very emotional and psychological characteristics that set us apart from men, we are designed by God to nurture and nourish others. It is not only what we have been shaped to do; many women want to be nurtured but are afraid to ask, and you may long to nurture them but don't know how.

CALLED TO MINISTER CARE AND NURTURING

The call to minister to another woman is one of the most significant commands to women in the New Testament. Ministry is not a status, reserved for an elite few, for only men or only women. It is a function of every member of the body of Christ. You may not think your care or nurture quotient is very high. In fact, many woman have said to me, "My husband is a better nurturer than I am." Although that may be true for you, it is not a good enough reason to not care for the women God puts in your life. Listen to what women are saying:

"Women should minister to women because our common emotional bond can provide the bridge we need to share our love for God with each other."

"Women need to nourish women because we need the fellowship, friendships and godly example. Plus, we have a good time doing it!" (Julie Born)

"Women should serve each other because we listen from the heart to each other. We show compassion."

"Women are often empathetic in a way a man may not be. I need that dimension in my life."

"Women need to come together to nurture each other because society tells us we must be supermoms and strong businesswomen. We may be that on occasion but more often, women get lost in the need of affirmation and validation. Bible study is a saving grace for all women who are willing to sit still and be nurtured by another woman!"

WHY YOU CAN NURTURE OTHERS

There are at least three reasons that you are designed by God to nurture other women. The first is *an ultimate purpose:* to know God. Jesus tells us in John 17:3 that this is the definition of eternal life: "Now this is eternal life: that they may know you, the only true God, and Jesus Christ, whom you have sent." It is the ultimate purpose for which Jesus came. We now share that purpose with Him. Second, Paul says we share *a common purpose* with all believers, and that is that we would be transformed to look like Christ (2 Corinthians 3:18) and conduct ourselves as He did: by serving others (Philippians 2:1–11). As we set our hearts to follow Him, we discover that He has *an individual purpose* for us: to be uniquely who God intends each one of us to be. Paul confirms that in Ephesians 2:10 when he says, "We are God's workmanship, created in Christ Jesus to do good works, which God prepared in advance for us to do." Our individual purpose then must include being in the place where God directs us and discovering the tasks He chooses for us.

Because of your general design as a woman and your particular personal and spiritual configuration, you are richly endowed to nurture, to relate emotionally and spiritually with women in your local church and circle of friends.

A helpful way to discover how prepared you are by God to nurture those women in your life is to take a look at your personal "design." In chapter 5, we pursued the idea of the mandate of mentoring other women. In this chapter, we will focus on how God has prepared us to care for one another. We learn what that means by looking at the ministry of the Holy Spirit of God.

The Holy Spirit Nurtures Us by Cultivating Our Hearts

What does it mean to nurture another woman? The *American Heritage Dictionary* defines the word *nurture* as "to foster, to cultivate." Anyone who grows a garden knows the importance of tending the ground in order for the plant or seed to grow. It is the kind of thing the Old Testament prophets promised would happen to Israel's stony heart because of the New Covenant. You remember what hard hearts the Israelites had in the wilderness. They were grumblers and complainers; some of them never enjoyed the Promised Land because they grumbled against God. Repeatedly, Moses wanted to throw up his hands in frustration because they were a hard bunch to lead. Many years after the wilderness generation was dead and gone, after the kingdom had collapsed and the people were taken to Babylon in exile, Ezekiel spoke of a new day. He talked about the Spirit transforming us from the inside out so we become like a well-cultivated garden, bearing fruit for others to enjoy. It is what the Holy Spirit does for us as He prepares our hearts to receive the Word of God and believe on Jesus. Listen to Ezekiel as he explains God's work through the Spirit: "I will sprinkle clean water on you. . . . I will cleanse you from all your impurities. . . . I will give you a new heart and put a new spirit in you; I will remove from you your heart of stone and give you a heart of flesh. And I will put my Spirit in you and move you to follow my decrees" (Ezekiel 36:25–27).

This is the privilege we now enjoy daily under the new covenant because of the death and resurrection of the Lord Jesus (Matthew 26:28). Our hearts have been cultivated, softened, and readied to receive God's Word by the Holy Spirit (2 Corinthians 3:3). James, the half brother of Jesus, explains it in the context of the Word of truth. He says that believers have been born again through the Word. Because of that, he says in his first chapter, "Everyone should be quick to listen, slow to speak and slow to become angry. . . . Get rid of all moral filth and the evil that is so prevalent and humbly accept the word planted in you, which can save you" (James 1:19–21).

The Holy Spirit nurtures us by cultivating our hearts and preparing them to receive God's Word. The Holy Spirit fosters an atmosphere of growth and care. John the apostle uses the Greek word *paraclete* and says the Spirit is the Helper, the Counselor, the One who comforts us. It is a beautiful truth and rich in hope as we understand that the root of that word means He comes alongside us and makes the journey bearable (John 14:15–21).

Why is the Holy Spirit, the third person of the Trinity, so able to nurture us? Because He is designed to care for us. He fosters love in our hearts so we respond to and obey the Savior, as Peter teaches in 1 Peter 1:2. He reminds us that we are "chosen according to the foreknowledge of God the Father, through the sanctifying work of the Spirit, for obedience to Jesus Christ and sprinkling by his blood." He sets us apart for purposes far greater than we can imagine. He cultivates the soil of our inner soul so we receive the implanted Word. Why should we give that same kind of ministry to other women? Because we are fitted to nurture women, designed by God to carry out the task.

Your DESIGN Enables You to Nurture Others

We all have within us deep desires, heart-concerns that move us in certain directions in life. Scripture says God works within us to will and to act according to His good purposes (Philippians 2:13). These inner yearnings to serve Christ reveal a great deal about who we are. Do not underestimate this task of nurturing women. If you catch even a little glimpse of this ministry you will never be the same again. God has made you in such a way that you may function as a nurturer in the community of believers. As you answer the questions raised using the acronym DESIGN, begin to ask God to soften your heart and show you how to come alongside other women. The answers you give may become those very things that God wishes to use as a cultivating tool in another woman's life.

D = DESIRES. The D in **DESIGN** stands for DESIRES. Desires motivate and delight us. They get us out of bed in the morning. In order to identify the desires God has put in your heart, ask yourself the following questions in the light of our discussion on nurturing and caring for women.

1. What do I *love* to do for Jesus?
   (This is my *passion* because I have done it and the joy lingers.)
2. What do I *want* to do for Jesus?
   (This is my *dream* because I can see the potential for service.)
3. What do I *need* to do for Jesus?
   (This is my *burden* because I cannot get it out of my mind.)
4. What do I *see* to do for Jesus?
   (This is my *vision* because I see it when others don't.)
5. What do I *delight* to do for Jesus?
   (I have great inner *satisfaction* when I do this for Him.)
6. What do I *think* God intends me to do?
   (This is my *calling* in life, and others have confirmed that to me.)

You will recognize your desires by the answers to the questions. As you answer them, think of what you would love to be doing in ministry for women in five years, in ten years. As you evaluate these desires, ask yourself if they reflect the highest and best God has placed in you. How did these desires develop within? Are they a result of God's calling? Family or church values? Habits you have developed?

E = EXPERIENCES. The E in D**E**SIGN refers to important EXPERI-
ENCES you have had in your life. Looking back is often the best way to
move ahead. As you see how you have developed from birth to the present, you often see patterns that bear the fingerprints of God on your life.
Take the time to fill in the following instructions.

1. See your life as a whole. A very useful tool to help you look at your
   life in a glance is something called a life-map. Whether you use a
   timeline or descriptive picture (metaphor) to portray the growth of
   your spiritual life, review your life noting the following.
   a. The key events
   b. The significant people
   c. Important personal experiences
2. Watch the strands come together. Like finely woven fabric, your life
   is composed of many strands that come together in beauty. In a single
   phrase, jot down (or tell the person with whom you are reading this
   book) how each of the following life experiences affected or shapes
   your life.
   a. Relational experiences—family and important friends
   b. Spiritual experiences—rebirth, important lessons, joys, sorrows,
      memorable spiritual encounters
   c. Educational experiences—courses of study, influential teachers
   d. Vocational experiences—significant jobs and tasks
   e. Ministry experiences—positive and negative, formal and informal
   f. Painful experiences—growth-related pains that have shaped you,
      pains you have resolved
3. Evaluate your experiences.
   a. What pattern has developed in the way you have responded over
      time?
   b. What spiritual problems or challenges are yet unresolved?

S = STRENGTHS (SKILLS). The S in D**E**S**I**GN stands for STRENGTHS
or natural skills and abilities God's grace has given you. When you have these
strengths clear in your mind, you will be more able to come alongside someone who can benefit from them. Since we did not earn these skills, it is foolish to glory in them proudly. But God gives good gifts and expects us to
use them for the good of others. The following will help us better understand our strengths.

WOMEN ARE NATURAL NURTURERS 139

1. We have natural talents because of Creation (see Genesis 1:27). Made in God's image, we have inherent abilities. Circle the following words that describe your strengths.

    a. verbal   b. physical   c. artistic/musical/creative

    d. mechanical   e. studious

2. We acquire skills by Learning. In how many of the above categories have you acquired skills by learning?

3. We increase our competence by evaluating and prioritizing. Evaluate yourself on the following:

    a. I *like* to work with people, things/tasks, or data/information/ideas.

    b. *Others say* I work best with people, things/tasks, or data/information/ideas.

    c. I am *most effective* when I work with people, things/tasks, or data/information/ideas.

4. We develop confidence as we know our personal strengths. You may have undiscovered, underused, and underdeveloped strengths. Here are the signs of a strength.

    a. I have a sense of satisfaction when I do it.

    b. I use the skill naturally or the learned skill easily.

    c. It is an area in which I have a record of accomplishment. (List one.)

    d. People are encouraged when I use this skill.

    e. I am at my best when I use this skill.

    f. I am energized when I use this skill.

5. We stay credible when we recognize our personal liabilities. Scripture is full of people who have to come to grips with their flaws: for example Naomi (Ruth 1:20–21), David (2 Samuel 12), Peter (Matthew 16:21–23; 26:31–46). Had they not recognized their weaknesses, they would never have been used by God in the area of their strengths. Here are some important distinctions.

    a. Weaknesses are perpetual areas of struggle and difficulty. (Can you list one?)

    b. Limitations are gifts, talents, and abilities you don't have. (List one.)

    c. Flaws are areas of moral or spiritual failure that must be changed. (List at least one.)

NOTE: The solution to staying credible with those you are nurturing in Christ is to be transparent and remember this:

    a. Maximize your strengths. (Focus and build.)

    b. Manage your weaknesses. (Recognize and monitor.)

      c. Accept your limitations. (Realize and release to the Lord.)

      d. Attack your flaws. (Ruthlessly refuse to indulge them.)

I = IDENTITY. The I in DESIGN refers to IDENTITY. Each of us is a complex combination of behavioral traits, emotional patterns, and thought processes. The result, however, is a distinctive personality and temperament that makes us who we are. This is obvious to parents who have more than one child. They quickly become aware of how different each of their children is from the others. Psychologists debate how much of our personality is inherent and how much acquired from our surroundings. Even as the Lord refines and transforms our character, our basic personality type is rarely altered.

    There are many widely used and helpful personality surveys that help you discern your basic personality traits. Although they may lead to self-absorption, they can help you to assess yourself. They require careful evaluation. If you want a resource that describes the Myers-Briggs Personality Test, *Please Understand Me* by Keirsey and Bates (Prometheus Publ., 1978) will help you. A close study of the twelve disciples will give you insight into differences and leadership. My all-time favorite discussion of differing personalities is still found in the Winnie the Pooh community.

    The important thing here is that you understand your temperament, which may be described with words like introvert, extrovert, thinker, feeler, intuitive, sensitive, perceiver, judger. Every single one of us is a mix, and we all stand in need of transformation. In recognizing who we are, we cannot make excuses that indulge our personal comfort, but instead can see our weaknesses as areas where we have to work harder to be effective.

G = GIFTS. The G in DESIGN refers to your spiritual GIFTS. If you compare a herd of buffalo and a flock of geese, you discover that buffalo, or bison, are powerful creatures. They are very loyal to their leader; they will do what their leader does and go wherever he goes. But when the head buffalo is absent or inactive, the others stand around and wait. On the other hand, as you observe geese, you will see that when they fly, they fly in formation. They operate interdependently. They share the task of leading, and every goose has a role to play, serving both as leader and follower.

    Using these analogies, the local church where you minister is meant to be far more like a flock of geese than a herd of buffalo. It is a shared task, not a one-man job. The church as an organism is built on interdependence, and that interdependence is based on the biblical concept of spiritual gifts. You may find the list in four passages: Romans 12; 1 Corinthians 12; Ephesians 4; and 1 Peter 4. The purpose of this book is not to define and discuss the variety of spiritual gifts and how you may use them as the means by which you nurture and care for the women in your local church. It is enough to clarify this: A spiritual gift is a special ability, given by the Holy Spirit to a believer, which enables each believer to edify others so the body of Christ is built up and strengthened. Gifts are sovereignly given by the Head of the church (1 Corinthians 12:4, 7), and their purpose is to glorify God (1 Peter 4:11) for the common good of the body (1 Corinthians 12:7) and for the growth and building up of the body. They are never given for self-edification (1 Corinthians 14).

As you seek to minister in the body of believers, make your priority the SMARTS we spoke of earlier. At the end of the day when you meet the Savior, you will give an account of your life. The thing He will reward His children for primarily is the intimate relationship the believer and He enjoyed. His words to Martha about Mary are still binding: "She has chosen the better part [she listened to the Savior], and it shall not be taken away from her." He will then look for how you served His purposes. Mary again is the shining example as she pours out her treasure, her alabaster vial of pure nard, anointing Him before His burial (John 12:3). And Martha joins the ranks of those who use their gifts with joy (Luke 10:38–41). In my husband's book *Life in His Body,* he suggests four things to help you find your spiritual gift.

1. Understand first how Scripture describes the gifts. Then ask, Who in the New Testament modeled these? How were they practiced?
2. Try out some things, getting involved in ministry wherever you can. You will not know what you cannot do until you try. Evaluate yourself after you have tried—does this fit with your desires? Did God bless what you did? Don't be afraid to do it badly. As you practice, the Holy Spirit will teach you to do it well.
3. Ask others for confirmation of what you did. Were you encouraged, strengthened, comforted by this?
4. Continue to develop the gifts, looking for every opportunity to use them. Use them when no one is looking. She who is faithful in a little will be faithful in a lot![1]

N=NATURE. The N in DESIG**N** refers to NATURE. When we talk about our nature in this context, we are not referring to the sinful nature of man. We are stepping back to get some perspective on who we are. It includes many issues already discussed and focuses on the big picture. It is saying, "Oh, that's *just* like Mary to do that!" or "That's *exactly* what Joan would do in these circumstances!" when we hear what Mary or Joan is doing or saying or how she is serving.

I have a friend named Lucy who has often come to retreats with me, praying for me as I speak and mingling with women over meals. Inevitably, during a weekend retreat, I will catch a glimpse of Lucy as she is helping to pick up whatever needs to be done. No one had to sit her down and walk her through the task; she saw what needed to be done and just did it. She is the closest to a genuine servant in the body of Christ I have ever seen. When it comes to certain needs of women in our church or tasks in our events, we know exactly where Lucy fits, with whom Lucy connects. That's because we know Lucy's identity! A few months ago, Lucy and her husband had a chance to return to Indonesia where they had served with Missionary Aviation Fellowship years earlier. The agency needed her husband to come and do some tidying up of financial matters. No one was surprised that Lucy was excited to go.

Your identity refers to certain values and behaviors that so clearly characterize you that your friends can describe your characteristic traits to others. God created you with specific, recognizable traits and skills that are a fundamental part of who you are. Use these final questions to help you recognize your own identity before God.

1. What would I do willingly and joyfully for the Lord Jesus no matter where in the world I was, given discretionary time? Despite my job description in life, what are some things that continue to motivate me even when the work is difficult?
2. How would my three best friends describe me?

THINK IT OVER

1. How have you organized your daily life so the priority of knowing the Lord Jesus intimately is possible?

2. What opportunities do you see for nurturing women in the circle of relationships in the body of believers where God has placed you?

3. What are you thankful for in the way God has fashioned you? How has this enabled you to serve Him?

4. What opportunities with women in your local church do you see God opening up because of your DESIGN?

5. What are you willing to ask the Lord to do with you so you can function the way He intends you to function?

THINK IT THROUGH

Take a look at the Proverbs 31 woman in the context of nurturing relationships. Read the chapter, and then, on a clean sheet of paper, list all the relationships this woman cultivates and nurtures. What is the effect on her household?

Take the time to read Ephesians 4:25–32 to understand the tools God would have you use as you seek to nurture other women to be soft and usable for the Lord Jesus. Resolve what you can do for others from this passage and ask God to help you do it.

NOTE

1. Gary Inrig, *Life in His Body* (Wheaton, Ill,: Harold Shaw, 1998), 14.

Chapter Ten

WOMEN ARE CALLED TO BE PRAY-ERS

"I have a wonderful friend who has had quite an influence on my life. She is more than twenty-five years older than me and is like a mother, friend, and mentor all in one! One of the main things she has taught me is the importance of prayer. I know this woman prays for me all the time, a comfort to know. I have learned from her to pray more for others."

"My Aunt Heidi prayed for me every day from the day I was born to the day she died. I'll never know the full impact of her consistent prayers in my life."

"Working with other women in ministry results in deeper and intimate relationships, especially in prayer. When we pray the prayers of the Bible for each other, we grow in at least two ways: We begin to look more like God and we begin to act more like Him too in the way we serve others!"

"I teach women in our church to pray the same way I taught our children how. 'Don't get fancy. Don't go long. Follow the Master Pray-er. Take the Disciples' Prayer (also known as the Lord's Prayer) and include in your prayer time what He included.' We are on safe ground when we pray like He prayed."

ELIZABETH INRIG, Women's Ministries

"We know people say they pray. But as needs come up in the lives of those in our local church, the seventy women in the Prayer Clusters pass on the message and pray. They don't share their opinions or ask unnecessary questions. They just pray. And God is answering our prayers."

KATHY STINSON, Prayer Cluster Coordinator,
Women's Ministries

WOMEN ARE CALLED TO BE PRAY-ERS

For many years, I prayed the child's prayer:

> *"Now I lay me down to sleep, I pray the Lord my soul to keep.*
> *If I should die before I wake. I pray the Lord my soul to take."*

Following that prayer, I would add a simple, "Bless mother, daddy, this one, that one . . ." Before you give me credit for remembering the prayer (or withhold it because I was too old to be praying it!), I wish I had learned sooner the importance of prayer in my life. The thought of praying out loud *with* someone terrified me. The idea of praying an adult prayer eluded me.

My pygmy-sized prayer life was in no way due to my parents' lack of praying. Both of them prayed. Each of them prayed daily. One of my earliest childhood memories of my father was his kneeling at the sofa in the living room with his Bible open, praying before he left for work in the morning. He believed that to open any book or newspaper before he first met with the Lord was a mistake. So he rose early in the morning to spend his first minutes with God.

Every evening at dinnertime, my father led us in Scripture reading and family prayer. Father prayed, but we did not pray aloud together in our home. Sunday mornings, as one of our church's teaching elders, if my father stood in our local church to thank God for the gift of His Son, there was no doubt in my mind that my father knew God well.

Though I rarely heard my mother pray aloud, I always knew she prayed and valued prayer. She told me when I was just a little girl how at eighteen, after she had trusted Christ, she loved to go to prayer meetings. She modeled that all my life. Her normal personal pattern at night was similar to my father's in the morning. Any night of the week just before bed her children could find her on her knees with her Bible open at the side of the bed, praying to the Father. On certain occasions if things were hard in her life, I would find her sitting at two or three in the morning in the middle of the kitchen, crying out to God with her Bible on her lap. Although I didn't always like to take the time, I will forever be thankful that my mother always prayed with me before I left for school in the morning, entrusting me to the Father's care.

I never wondered that my parents believed they *should* pray. Prayer shaped the way they lived their Christian lives. And they never questioned God's *right* to call them into His presence. They only knew to obey. I think my mother prayed on occasion with her friends. But, looking back, I did wonder what my parents said when they were alone with God. I think they would not be as concerned about magical prayer formulas as some are today. They would solemnly urge us to read Matthew 7:21 where the Lord says, "Not everyone who *says* to me, 'Lord, Lord,' will enter the kingdom of heaven, but only he who *does* the will of my Father who is in heaven" (italics added). They would caution the view that words are what God is looking for and urge us to take an inventory on our heart, whether it is obedient to the Father's will.

Here's a practical way to learn to pray from the Master Pray-er. Let's look briefly at what is commonly called the Lord's Prayer.

Our Father
> Call God *Father.* Don't just call Him *God!* He is your Father if you know His Son Jesus as your Savior.

Who is in heaven
> *Honor Him alone.* He is in charge of the universe. Not one star in the heavens or one detail of your life is out of His sight. He knows.

Holy is your Name
> *Fear and respect Him alone.* He is kind, gracious, just, merciful, forgiving —it's time to remember the power behind the holy name of God whose Son is the Lord Jesus Christ, Savior, Messiah, Redeemer, Deliverer . . .

Your Kingdom come
> *Remember His purposes* are on a far grander scale than yours. He is working everything toward the climax in history when His Son will rule over lesser kingdoms as King of kings and Lord of lords. Live for His kingdom.

Your will be done on earth
> God's will is "good, pleasing and perfect" (Romans 12:2). Pray for a heart that submits to His plans and obeys His ways. God's Word is where

you find His will stated and getting done, just as it is being done in heaven. Pray this for yourself and all those on your prayer list.

Give us today's bread

Today is the time He has promised to meet your needs. Don't get greedy for tomorrow. Ask for strength and blessing for today. He is a generous provider. Who needs His bread today?

Forgive us our sins

Confession and repentance are the key to answered prayers and a happy heart (1 John 1:9).

As we forgive

Grace and forgiveness are the key to credible relationships and a happy home and church.

Lead us not into temptation

Knowing where you tend to sin is the key to staying away from temptation.

Keep us safe from evil

The Enemy of our souls is defeated. There is no need to give him special attention. A simple "deliver us from the evil one" is enough. We are not under the foe's control (Colossians 2:13–15 and 1 John 5:18–19). Christ is our Victor. Talk to Him.

WORDS ARE NOT ENOUGH

Before we discuss the priority of growing praying women in the local church, there is an important issue to address about multiplying words in prayer. In a day when the political climate insists on "freedom of speech," Scripture challenges that thinking both in how we speak to each other (Ephesians 4:25–32) and the way we use words to address God. It is helpful to examine the relationship God establishes between words and deeds. It is different from the thinking of those who believe that if we get more people to pray and more prayers to be said, if we *declare* we want revival and *call* the church to revival, God is obligated to bring revival. There is a subtle belief (sometimes not so subtle) that the power of prayer is found in *the number of words* or *the pattern of words used* to call on God. Scripture never relates answers to prayer on quantity or formula. In fact it teaches not a formula or a structure but a conversation based on relationship. Jesus warned His disciples not to pray like hypocrites who stood on the corners of the streets and prayed "to be seen by men" (Matthew 6:5). He cautioned them not to pray like the pagans, "who keep on babbling . . . for they think they will be heard because of their many words" (v. 7). Scripture's order is op-posite to the order of the day: James gives us the principle for powerful prayer at the end of his book when he says, "The prayer of a righteous man is powerful and effective." His example is Elijah, one person called to prophesy to the Baal-worshiping northern kingdom of Israel. Elijah did not call the nation to a prayer meeting. He modeled obedience to them by declaring the Lord is God. Then he prayed as one righteous man on behalf of individuals (1 Kings 17:19–24) and the nation (1 Kings 18:20–39). Elijah's prayers are short and effective! In fact, apart from Solomon's dedi-catory prayer of the temple (2 Chronicles 6:12–42) most of the prayers in the Bible can be prayed in a matter of seconds and some in a handful of minutes (for example, see Hezekiah's prayer in Isaiah 37:15–20). There may be a time for long seasons of prayer, but public prayers particularly should be short and purposeful.

MODELS OF PRAYERS MATTER

Therefore the models of praying people in the Bible are important. As Scripture teaches, the believer does not become a spiritual person by praying. Those who pray best pray as an extension of their relationship to the Lord, which, of course, they gain partly by coming to know Him through prayer. They are already in a spiritually dependent relationship with God. As women of this age, we can reach the potential of those who prayed in Scripture when our prayer life is an extension of our longing to know God. We take our cue from the Bible, not the pagans around us. This keeps the style and effectiveness of our prayers, and the length of public prayers, consistent with the Lord's order for Christian living from the instruction in the Sermon on the Mount. It is James's perspective on effectual prayer.

You will find the same principle taught by Paul in all his letters: The natural overflow of the spiritually passionate heart is obedience to the will of the Father in His Word, out of which flows the joyful obligation and responsibility to pray. The Lord Jesus intends women to develop prayer as a lifestyle rather than making it an event. He wants us to multiply deeds of obedience and kindness rather than multiplying our words. Godly praying without godly living is impossible. Behaving obediently precedes prevail-ing prayer. The multiplying of spiritual words, the rote speech of memo-rized but meaningless prayers, the repeated warfare formulas do not ring true to Scripture. It is as hard to convince a lukewarm Christian heart to pray without ceasing as it is for an untrained athlete to run a marathon. Paul's model of prayer requests and praying are simple, uncomplicated, and the product of passion for the Lord Jesus Christ (see 2 Thessalonians 3:1–5).

Many of the women with whom I've sat over the years in small groups are women like I was in earlier years: afraid to pray out loud. Afraid of what others might think of my stuttering prayers. Afraid to admit a prayer need in case no one else understands. By the time I was praying with women, I had learned to do two things: Find the women who were known to be pray-ers, and pray with them. If I was unsure of my prayers, I wrote them on three-by-five cards and read them. I had learned that as a young nineteen-year-old from the man who would be my husband. As our relationship grew, he believed if we prayed at the end of our dates, we would not succumb to the temptations of the flesh. I agreed. Though this wasn't a magic cure-all (we weren't pushing the limits in our dating behavior and assuming a quick prayer would protect us), it kept us conscious of God's presence in our relationship. But because praying aloud was personally threatening, I read my prayers while Gary's eyes were shut. For a while, I also did that when I prayed with women.

The more I practiced the heart language of the Christ follower in speaking to God, the less threatened I became to pray aloud. After I married and began to grow as a Christian, God never failed to put women in my life who were valiant prayer warriors. They modeled faithful prayerfulness and consistently and often spontaneously, at any given moment and for every reason, prayed! Even as I write these words, I remember who they are, where they live. I know them not as those who argue with God about why we should pray but as those who model the humble spirit characteristic of women of prayer.

PRAYER IS OXYGEN FOR YOUR SPIRITUAL LIFE

Learning to pray is one of the most important skills you will ever need as a woman who is a Christ follower. Learning to pray with women for their needs and families, their neighborhoods and churches, is a luxury your life cannot afford to be without. As oxygen is indispensable to the lungs, so prayer is indispensable to our spiritual life. It is the necessary spiritual oxygen that keeps your relationship with the triune God alive and intimate. It is shortsighted to think that prayer is an event, a weekend away where you go to pray. The goal for the praying Christ follower is to learn to breathe without ceasing. It is this that Paul gives us insight into when he commands the Thessalonians in 1 Thessalonians 5:16–18, "Be joyful always; pray continually; give thanks in all circumstances." Why? "For this is God's will for you in Christ Jesus."

Women who have learned to pray don't hold their spiritual breath, waiting for the evening. *They learn* to breathe in the daily and weekly rhythms of their spiritual lives. *They evaluate* the busyness of their day. *They decide* how they will build into their twenty-four hours a dependency on the Lord. Like people who are alive, *they use their spiritual breath to aid them in every kind of activity.* As time passes, they learn the skill of taking time to stop and rest in the same way they would recoup following a hard walk or an intense task. Women who are known to be pray-ers pray because they have discovered it is God's will, not because they have gone to a prayer seminar. They are convinced of the joyful obligation they have as living spiritual beings to cry out in praise to God, to repent before Him, to depend on Him, and to pray with and intercede on behalf of others. And the women who do that see God's glory as He answers their prayers!

TEACH US TO PRAY

God's Word is clear about the teaching of prayer. It teaches us why, when, how, and what to pray. In fact, the only thing the disciples ever asked the Lord Jesus to teach them is recorded in Luke 11:1. Matthew includes this prayer as part of the Sermon on the Mount (Matthew 6). Luke does not tell us the occasion when the disciples asked to be taught to pray, whether Jesus had been on the mountain praying with the Father (something He did on a regular basis in the rhythm of His life), which might have piqued their attention and elicited the question. He only says the disciples wanted to learn in the same way John's disciples had learned from him.

Jesus answered by giving them a pattern on which they can model their own prayers. It is a simple prayer but profound because it includes the kind of conversation someone can have who wants to build a relationship with God. It reflects the kind of prayer common to both Old and New Testaments.

WOMEN ARE KNOWN TO BE PRAY-ERS

Women from the past have been known to be pray-ers. Before the church existed, Hannah in her distress pleaded with Yahweh to open her womb (1 Samuel 1:1–15). In her new friendship with the Lord Jesus, Mary of Bethany listened humbly to what the Lord Jesus had to say just days before His death (John 12). After the birthday of the church (Acts 2), one of the activities the men and women devoted themselves to was prayer. In Acts 16, Luke tells us that God-fearing women like Lydia gathered for prayer. It is there at the riverside in Philippi that Paul found these women. They listened to his message and trusted in the Lord for salvation.

Over the centuries as the church has flourished, women have called on the name of the Lord. At the turn of the twentieth century in Wales, two Welsh women sat at their kitchen table and pleaded with God for revival in their country. The Welsh Revivals effected the change of a nation as men and women repented of their sins. In our day, movements like Moms in Touch draw women together to pray for their most precious assets: their children in school.

Why Do Women Pray Together?

When women come together to pray, several principles help. First, God's Word should be read as the needs and concerns are shared. That way, you will always have God's perspective on your prayers. Second, prayer itself should be a priority. When requests are shared in detail, there is often no time left for prayer. If you are praying as a group from your local church, the leader must model careful time management. I believe a primary way women make a difference in other women's lives is to pray together. When you really pray for each other and the concerns you have, you will not simply have fellowship (*koinonia*) with the Father: You will have fellowship with each other, which is evidence of the filling of the Holy Spirit of God (see Ephesians 5:18–21 and Colossians 3:15–17).

Why Should Women Pray?

Prayer is one of the most important things women can do together. I have discovered even with my friends who do not yet know the Lord Jesus Christ personally, their deep appreciation for prayer. When life is hard, they call and ask for prayer. What a gift to those who need to know our God hears His children when they cry. What a delight to see Him answer prayer on their behalf. Never underestimate your ability as a woman to pray with another woman and for other women. If the godly women of the Bible were praisers (Exodus 15:21) and pray-ers (1 Samuel 1 and Luke 1:46–55), why should we not be? For your encouragement, the following answers are for those of you who, like many women in my life, have repeatedly asked, "Why pray?"

We pray because prayer is the means by which we get to know the Father (John 14:9–21). We pray because prayer to Christ followers is like breath to the human being. We cannot grow without it. We cannot communicate apart from it. We pray because we are commanded to pray (1 Thessalonians 5:17), and when we pray, it pleases the Father because it is His will for us (v. 18). We pray to fulfill our responsibility toward others (1 Samuel 12:23). We pray so the name of the Lord Jesus is glorified and lifted up in the life of every believer (2 Thessalonians 1:12).

How Can Women Pray?

When should we pray? Scripture answers that as well. We pray at all times. For whom should we pray? We pray for all people. We pray for our government and leaders. For what should we pray? We pray for all needs, especially that which is necessary to fulfill our part in God's plan (1 Thessalonians 3:9–13; 5:16–17). The most liberating things happen when we pray according to the will of God as recorded in Scripture. We pray for God's glory, honor, and holiness to be revealed on the earth; for God's kingdom to come; and for His will to be done on earth. We pray for our daily bread, for forgiveness and repentance for our sin, for resistance to sin, and for protection from evil and the Evil One. Paul encourages us to make every anxious thought a reason to pray (Philippians 4:4–8). He says this can be done by releasing the worries to the Lord in prayer, asking for requests with a thankful heart. The promise is not that we get what we want but that we get what God will always give: peace that passes understanding and that guards our hearts and minds in the process! Paul is transparent about his prayer life, and he has three distinct prayer requests as he serves the Lord Jesus. He asks that people he meets will have open hearts, that on his journeys God will give him open doors, and that when he speaks the truth, he will be given an open mouth.

Nothing said in Scripture releases us from praying. Everything in Scripture compels us to treat prayer as the priority means by which we come to know the Father and His Son the Lord Jesus Christ through the power of the Holy Spirit.

Start Small—on Your Own. Intimacy with the Father is not based on a program or related to fancy performance. It is not even saying the right words so much as it is being the right person. Just as you build your human relationships, so resolve to build your spiritual relationship with the Father. Start small. Set aside time to listen to the Father speak to you through His Word. If you are a young mother, start with five to fifteen minutes. Turn off the television, your radio, or your music, and deal with anything else that might distract you, as though an honored dignitary has come to get to know you. He is the Lord of the universe and wants to enjoy a relationship with you if you will only take the time. If your little ones are tugging at your skirt, find a closet, a room, or space alone where you can be quiet and can meet the Lord Jesus for a moment. Tell your children you are meeting with the most important Person in the world. They can learn to respect your time with Him just as they do with any other of your friends. If you are at a different stage of life and have more discretionary time, set some of that time aside. Sit quietly and deliberately read God's Word as you would read a letter from a loving Father to His child. Think about what you've read. As you do, speak about the ideas He has communicated to you. It is there, in the "closet," that you build a foundation for prayer and a growing relationship with God. What you practice well in private will be done with ease in public.

Keep Going. Set aside these moments every day. No friendship can flourish without time and loyalty. Be alert as you read the passage you have chosen, being ready to hear God's Word. As you read, take the concerns of your heart with you. Name them there in the closet and leave them with the Father. He is kind. He loves you (John 14:21). He will not deceive you or change for the worse like others around you. He longs to share your life and show you what He is doing (James 1:16–18). He is willing to do for you what you cannot do for yourself (Matthew 7:7–12) and is looking to support those whose hearts are completely His (see 2 Chronicles 16:9).

When I was a young mother with three children under four years old, intimate moments with the Lord were hard to make. I discovered that if I filled a picnic basket with things to aid my time with the Lord, I had a plan to be ready to meet with Him. The items in my prayer basket were things I might include were I to fellowship with a friend. I included a cup for coffee or tea, a journal, my Bible and current study, note cards, a candle, and sometimes a linen cloth to set the things on—anything that signified the importance of the moment. As the children grew and left home, the basket remained a part of my early mornings. It became the help I needed to keep going and to anticipate with joy my time to meet with the Lord.

What Should Women Pray?

In a day when spirituality is a popular topic in circles not primarily Christian and when meditation is common, it is important to understand what the Bible means when it speaks about meditation and prayer. Meditation and prayer for the Christ follower is not emptying the mind of thoughts so much as it is bringing captive every thought to the mind of Christ. It is hearing the Father's thoughts as the Spirit has recorded them in His Word. It is understanding what He values in life. It is embracing the biblical worldview that permeates Scripture. It is the process of telling Him out loud that we have sinned, that we need to change, that we accept His Word as the only food that satisfies our inner souls. Most important, it is not simply agreeing with the prayer that two prayer partners pray so much as it is agreeing with God about what He has said in His Word.

Agree with God's Words. In its simplest description, prayer is *learning to adjust to God* and His will by *agreeing with Him.* Prayer is the gift God has given His children by which we may agree with Him. Just as I learned to adjust to my husband early on in our marriage, understanding our differences and accepting the changes, so as Christ followers we learn to adjust to the will and ways of God. The difference between adjusting to a new friend or city or job and adjusting to God is that He is always right! His standards are holy, and His purposes are eternal. His will and His desires for us as revealed in His Word are good and acceptable (Romans 12:1–2).

Yet in spite of all we know from what He says and what He wants, agreeing with Him is hard. We are so unlike Him! But to adjust to His character we must first agree, confess, that His is the final answer in the universe. To adjust to His ways goes against our human pride. To agree with His words will mean that we give up our own plans and choose His way. But once we resolve to agree with what He says, we are forever compelled to adjust our lives to His pleasure. It is through agreeing with Him in prayer that even the youngest Christ follower learns to listen to His Word and respond as an obedient child. Through knowing what He says in His Word, even the least fluent believer learns to speak the heart language of God.

Agree with Who He Is and Who We Are. The apostle John in 1 John 1:9 uses the word "confess" as he calls believers to admit who they are before God. In the context of warning those who say they have fellowship with God yet keep on sinning and walk in darkness, he says this: "If we confess our sins, he is faithful and just to forgive us our sins, and to cleanse us from all unrighteousness" (KJV).

John's concern for believers who fellowship together is not for whether we are seasoned or novice pray-ers. Nor is it whether as God's children, we will sin or not. All the children in God's family sin. The concern is whether or not as God's children we enjoy and appreciate our Advocate, Jesus Christ the righteous One. When we agree about our sin, we learn to adjust to the holy standards of God. We walk in the light and stay out of the dark. If we refuse to agree we have sinned, we never adjust to the likeness of Christ but remain in the dark.

The amazing thing in these verses is this: When we agree with God about our sin, He forgives us and cleans us up so we can adjust to Him. As you meet with your prayer partner or pray with women in your prayer group, let me suggest five things about which every Christian pray-er must learn to agree. Whether you are a seasoned or novice pray-er, you will never get over your need to agree with God in prayer on these.

Agree with God About HIMSELF. All spiritual wisdom begins when you first recognize *who* God is as revealed in His Word. From Genesis to Revelation, the writers of Scripture bear witness to God's awesome character and marvelous ways. The first place to start in any relationship with God is to first see *who* He is and *what* He is like. When you see Him for His beauty and glory, you respond in praise. This is worship. This is agreeing with God about His worthy character and holy actions. Many of the psalms and most of the prayers in the Bible begin by lifting high the name of the Lord.

Agree with God About HIS WORD. Spiritual growth and maturity come as you *daily accept* God's Word. There is no spiritual hormone or nutritional replacement, no spiritual fast food that feeds the soul of believers better than God's Holy Word. At the end of the day when we give account of our lives to the Lord Jesus, the only measure will be God's Word. You will not be measured against the best missionary, a godly author, or the pastor's wife who is your mentor. Your life will be held against the way in which you obeyed God's Word, not whether you agree with it.

Agree with God About YOURSELF. It is the task of the Holy Spirit to use Scripture to convict us and reveal to us our sin. When we agree with God about ourselves, we admit our sin and acknowledge His ability to forgive us. This is confession. As Christ followers, those who adjust to God's will in this way rejoice in the forgiveness of sin. We will never be perfect this side of heaven, but we should live a lifestyle of repentance.

Agree with God About YOUR BLESSINGS. It is not without purpose that Paul's words in Romans 1 expose the great sin of the twenty-first century (and all other centuries before) when he says those who suppress the truth are not thankful (Romans 1:21). Spiritual progress in your personal prayer life and prayer with others continues only as you personally and consistently appreciate God's goodness in your life. Paul will remind the Thessalonians and Philippians of this. The maturing believer adjusts to God by thanksgiving.

Agree with God About OTHERS' NEEDS. Spiritual strength and productivity increase as you intercede for others. One of the greatest ways of experiencing fellowship together as women is to pray for others. This is supplication (Philippians 4:6) and intercession. Praying for others is not a gift; it is expected of the woman who has learned to agree with God about the way He arranges His universe. Your family, your church, and your community need your prayers!

WOMEN WHO PRAY TOGETHER

Often we spend all our time praying for the last two items on the list above. The psalmist and others whose prayers are given in Scripture rarely do. Whether it is Hannah praying for a baby or Solomon dedicating the temple, whether it is Mary praising God's wisdom or Paul asking for prayer, all focus first on agreeing with God about who He is and what He has done in their lives. We learn from these saints how to pray. We learn for the spiritual health of our own families and local churches how important it is to first be a worshiper who submits to God's Word and repents, giving thanks always as we pray on behalf of others. In all of this, as you agree with God and His Word, you will find yourself adjusting more carefully in spirit, mind, and body to the will of God and His good pleasure.

As we learn to think and speak in a way that pleases the Father, we will know Him better and trust Him more. We will be known as those who have learned to call Him by His name, Father. We will learn how to say thank you and be known as those who seek to bless others by praying for them the truths we find in God's Word.

I'd like to close with some practical suggestions.

1. What kind of women should be praying?
   There are a number of qualifications God establishes for those who wish to be heard by God.

a. The one who is willing to admit her need (2 Chronicles 7:14)

b. The one who does not hold on to her sin (Psalm 66:18)

c. The one who believes Jesus is her only mediator (Hebrews 4:14–16)

d. The one who desires to share the gospel with others asks for three things: an open mouth (Ephesians 6:19), an open door (Colossians 4:3), and open hearts (2 Corinthians 6:11–12)

e. The one who is made righteous by faith (James 1:3–4; 5:16)

2. What things should women pray about?

In Scripture, we discover what you and I should pray about. We discover these by hearing what God's saints prayed and listening to the commands for prayer. The following will give you some ideas.

a. Confession of our sin (Matthew 6:12–13 and 1 John 1:9)

b. Our enemies, as David prays in the Psalms. Jesus also teaches this in Matthew 5:44 and 6:12, and 2 Thessalonians 1:5–10 speaks of its being God's decision as to *how* to deal with our enemies.

c. Our friends (Job 42:8 and Ephesians 1:15–23) and other believers (2 Thessalonians 3:1)

d. Praise for the Father's holiness, His will, our needs, protection from the Evil One, and the future (Matthew 6:9–12)

e. For those in authority over us (1 Timothy 2:1–2)

f. To be delivered from wicked and evil men (2 Thessalonians 3:2)

g. When there are no words for our needs (Romans 8:26)

THINK IT OVER

1. How do you arrange time for intimacy with the Father?

2. What do you use to keep going with your time with the Lord? What helps do you use to aid you?

3. Who are the women in your church known to be those who pray? What spiritual effect does their praying have on your church?

4. If you became an "agreer" with God so you can adjust to His person, His Word, His will, and His ways, what would need to change?

5. What difference would that make in your life? Your family's life? Your church's life?

THINK IT THROUGH

Here are some prayers you may want to pray from the Bible. You will never go wrong in prayer when you use the inspired Word as the substance for your prayers.

1. Ephesians 1:15–23
2. Colossians 1:9–12
3. 1 Thessalonians 3:11–13
4. 2 Thessalonians 1:11–12

PRACTICAL HELPS FOR BUILDING A THRIVING WOMEN'S MINISTRY

"When I choose to intentionally come and share in the experience of fellowship (koinonia) with the women who meet to study and pray, God begins a new work in my life. He continues it as I mingle with those who are not just women but women of the Spirit, not fighting women or performing women but women who practice submission of their spirit to this awesome King before they show up in public. The opportunity to experience this oneness of heart and purpose is the best!"

"I have used a devotional book for many years and never felt satisfied inside. I am learning as I commit to study God's Word weekly instead of people's words about the Word, that my mind is being changed and my heart is being challenged. I am really practicing Colossians 3:16 for the first time in my life!"

"The focus of Holy Scripture is my lifeline."

"When hard work is buttressed by good planning and serious praying, it shows by what God does in and through His children."

"I've wanted to accomplish so many 'good' things in my life. I now want to do God's things, whatever He asks of me."

Chapter Eleven

PRACTICAL HELPS FOR BUILDING
A THRIVING WOMEN'S MINISTRY

There is probably no culture more informed than ours. If we lack information on any subject, then books, videos, audios, and the Internet exist to tell us more about things than we would care to know.

Although understanding truth and being informed are important, no surface reader of the Scriptures can miss that God has invested His truth in the flesh of humanity. He did not run an ad in the heavens asking for disciples. He sent His Son who lived with men and women, "tabernacling" among us, communicating truth accompanied by touch and His very presence.

In the 1950s, Harry Harlow and his associates did some studies with infant monkeys that showed the importance of touch and warmth as the monkeys received their daily food. When given a choice of substitute mothers—a wire mesh "mother" constructed to hold a bottle or one that was covered or padded with terry cloth—the infant rhesus monkeys went to the softer mother, and they grew and thrived. Those who were left to be fed by a wire mesh "mother" deteriorated emotionally and physically and ultimately died because they received no tactile comfort. In other words, in the absence of real mothers, the infant monkeys consistently preferred mother substitutes that were soft and warm. They ignored the substitutes that provided no contact comfort in spite of their hunger for food.

Our need for nurturing—through touch, care, the willing use of a nurturing heart—is at the center of being a woman.

FIVE ESSENTIALS FOR BUILDING
A HEALTHY WOMEN'S MINISTRY

With the discovery of Bible study among women in the last fifty years, headed up by groups such as Christian Women's Clubs, Bible Study Fellowship, and Precept Ministries, came a new passion for God's Word.

Women flocked to homes. Churches lent their facilities out to different programs, while the women in the churches did not really know how to approach church leadership to start Bible studies in the church. Women were
uncertain as to how to stray from the procedures in place. In spite of some
confusion, women, hungry for God's Word, were learning at a new level
of understanding and growing in their walk with the Savior. For many years
I taught CWC Neighborhood Bible Studies in my neighborhood, cutting
my leadership teeth on their studies.

Sometime in the late 1970s, a few years after I began a women's Bible
study in our church in Calgary, a few ladies asked me to teach them how
to study the Bible. I was delighted to begin since anyone who has taken
Bible study methods from Howard G. Hendricks at Dallas Seminary leaves
the class believing every person he or she ever serves in any place *must* learn
principles of inductive Bible study.

So we began our trek through the notes. Eight of us met around a
huge boardroom table in the library of our church. Each session we carefully observed, interpreted, and applied God's truths. Our goal was to practice something we had learned that week before we returned for the next
week. They were good times. We dug up treasures we thought no one else
had ever seen and continued to focus on this in-depth study of the Word
for a few years.

That was many years ago now, and I still use the basis for inductive study
in my personal study and preparation of study materials for women in our
Bible study in California. But in the last thirty years, something began to
happen as I sat in small groups with women. The experiment I referred to
of Harry Harlow's and the rhesus monkeys began to live itself out in the
lives of the women I was teaching. The result is this: When we included
the nurturing aspects of Bible study, women came back. When we intentionally planned for the study to be a place where people prayed for each
other, women were consistent in their participation.

It is important to study God's Word. That is the center of our mission
statement. But the seed of God's Word takes root when there is a well wa-
tered, warmed soil in the heart. For pure nutrition to feed the cells in the
body, it must be in a setting of love and tenderness. It is how the Lord Jesus
treated His disciples and the multitudes. It is how the apostles handled the
early church, and it is the way growth of life works in a real world. It is not
enough to have good nutrition or to be well informed. It is not enough to
have good theology—it is just as important to have good behavior.

So, as a final encouragement to you to grow a healthy women's ministry, I would like to suggest there are five heart essentials for a healthy women's ministry to exist in a local church, five characteristics that do more than provide a program. They determine a course of action and are the basics, the backbone to a rich and thriving ministry to women. I would like to suggest that on their own, none of these basics will grow spiritually healthy women, just as no one activity in life produces physical health. Together, these five bring balance to ministry and provide the richness necessary for growth in women's ministries.

Fellowship and Friendship

Women enjoy having fellowship with each other. Since many of the important things the Lord Jesus taught were over a meal, we should learn the wisdom of growing a relationship as we linger over a cup of coffee. Eating together (without overindulging) can be a good prelude to the main purpose of the morning, evening, or occasion. Food has a wonderful way of allowing women to communicate and chat unhurriedly and spontaneously.

Praise

One of the things we know the Lord Jesus did with His disciples was to sing. Matthew and Mark both refer to the hymn Jesus sang with His disciples after He ate the Last Supper with them (Matthew 26:30 and Mark 14:26). Even before the early believers sang about Jesus, the Psalms existed as the great hymnbook of the Jewish nation. Singing to one another in psalms, hymns, and spiritual songs is one evidence of the filling of the Spirit in a believer's life (Ephesians 5:18–21). When women come together, there should be some time when the praise of God fills their hearts and minds and is on our lips. It softens the heart and prepares the mind for God's Word.

God's Word

The study of Scripture is the heartbeat of any thriving women's ministry. The study of Scripture is the control center because of the promises given to believers in Psalm 19:7–11. There is no substitute. You will not know personal transformation unless you personally, firsthand take Scripture into your life. But Scripture needs the context of relationship for its truth to sink in. When Jesus taught the disciples the truth, He lived with them—eating, walking, talking, fishing—for three years. After Paul went to Thessalonica, he says the people received and obeyed the Word gladly, and he reminds them of the context in which they did: He was like a mother and father, taking them to his very heart.

Any study of Scripture that is so academic that body life is absent misses the point of Bible study. The purpose of the study of Scripture is not simply to be better informed; it is to be transformed. Once you have studied God's Word, you have still only studied. It takes time and obedience to apply God's Word to your life in the manner of the early Christians. There is no value only in studying. The value is in being transformed!

Prayer

I believe that Bible study without prayer is not complete. And prayer without the Scripture being read is like praying in a vacuum. Most of the prayers of the Bible are very theocentric—God and Christ centered. The women who pray best pray with their Bibles open. And those who study without praying for each other lose the heart of applying God's Word to their lives. Prayer was never seen as the goal of the Christian life. It is the oxygen you breathe as you serve the Lord Jesus. It is never intended to be an event on its own. Not every verse in Scripture is about prayer. Relationship with Christ is the goal of the Christian life. The words of God are very words you learn to breathe, to pray as you live for the glory of God.

Good Works

You cannot read the Bible without recognizing that the call of God on our lives is to be servants. Good works are the evidence that God the Holy Spirit has made us spiritually alive. Romans and James teach us the importance of good works, not in contradictory ways but in complementary ways. Paul declares in Romans 3:25–26 that those who live by faith are justified. James 2:17 says that as a proof of salvation, faith must be seen by works. Faith without works is dead! So it is not ever really enough just to study the Bible alone as an exercise of the mind. You run the risk of getting a big head without growing a big heart. Those whose hearts are passionate about Scripture engage in good works. Bible study that functions at the center of a ministry in the local church should have a clear directive as to the good works the participants are carrying out. The normal and natural outpouring of a heart filled with God's Word is a desire to do good, to be busy doing good works for those in need. This is especially important in our day when self-absorption and greed become a pastime of those who should be doing good works and giving away.

A Closing Challenge

You can make a difference in your women's ministries. You can determine how the five essentials are woven throughout the ministry of women in your local church. When you intentionally plan to weave fellowship/friendship, praise, Bible study, prayer, and good works as threads throughout your ministry, you are well on your way to seeing the ground readied for a thriving women's ministry.

A WORD TO CHURCH LEADERS

*W*e prayed for sun and it rained the entire weekend! But as the 350 women flew from twenty-two states across the country to descend upon our church campus, there was an excitement in the air. It was the first "Equipping Celebration." For a number of years, I had discussed an idea with my National Women's Ministry team and local church women's ministry. We wanted to see what would happen in women's lives when we invited them to our church campus to be equipped for ministry in their local churches. We built our plans around the five heart essentials for a healthy women's ministry.

First, we would seek to create an atmosphere of acceptance and nurture by showing New Testament hospitality in our homes and on the campus. We wanted to use gracious touches to show every woman *she was loved and valued* in order to make this fellowship or *koinonia* become a reality.

Second, we would celebrate high praise. We wanted to corporately spend appropriate time to praise and worship the Lord our King. The women would be *asked to focus on the Lord Jesus Christ.*

Third, we would provide plenary sessions with a strong biblical focus on what it meant to be equipped to live for the King. The women would be *equipped for life and ministry by God's Word.*

Fourth, we would offer practical workshops to motivate and enable the women to carry out a ministry with women whether their church was large or small. They would have the opportunity to learn *how to serve.* They would also be asked to give of their substance to a worthy ministry to women.

Finally, we wanted to give every woman an opportunity to come in a new way and through prayer submit to the King of kings and Lord of lords. The women would be asked to *declare a new allegiance to the Lord Jesus,* letting go of things that might hold them back from serving with a whole heart.

The purpose was singular: We wanted to help women see how generously the Holy Spirit had equipped them to serve in their church to the glory of God.

Those involved in women's ministry in our church opened their hearts to the women. Almost one hundred families opened their homes for the weekend. As a special touch, I invited our elders and pastoral staff to join us during our first session, introducing them as the support team. I was amazed at the effect this simple act had on the women at the conference.

The truth is this: No women's ministry in any church can function without the wholehearted prayer and support of the men who are leaders of the church. The way the pastors and elders in my church value women deeply affects my ability to minister to women. Their public affirmation and support of women's ministries is a statement of trust and a gift beyond belief. It reflects the attitude of the Lord Jesus found in the Gospels (Luke 8:1–3). It mirrors Paul's comments in his letters where he emphasizes the partnership that men and women share in ministry in the church when they "work hard in the Lord" (Romans 16:12).

Up until now we have considered many reasons why women should minister to women in the context of the local church. Chapter 8 focused on Paul's charge to Titus, the pastor in Crete representing others who shepherd, to *teach sound doctrine*. As Titus does so, the church is equipped for spiritual health. Men and women are informed as to the role they have in this marvelous and mysterious body called the church. Older women, teaching what is good, are released by the local church to reach their spiritual potential and fulfill their God-given purpose.

As we begin this discussion, let me remind you that the times in which we live are like millennia past: There is nothing new under the sun (Ecclesiastes 1:9), and the human heart remains in desperate need to be regenerated. Sin is still sin. But something disturbing has occurred. For the past thirty years people in the church still took the difference between men and women for granted, while in the culture the difference was being dismantled. Now, caught in the wave of the feminist storm, some corners of the church have felt obliged to explain away God's arrangement of His way of doing things. And so a plethora of books has been written to adjust the thinking of how men and women should function in the church.

As recently as November 13, 2000, *Christianity Today* carried a report on a fast-growing American church that has erased any lines that might dare to separate the spiritual responsibilities of men from women as they serve in the church. Potential members joining this congregation must sign a statement committing themselves to "joyfully submit to the leadership of women in various leadership positions." The "various leadership positions" include those of teacher, preacher, and elder.[1] The problem with this statement is it removes the God-given mystery of distinctions for ministry roles to reflect a cultural bias and not the eternal purposes of God.

Women can more successfully serve women in the local church when there is a clear signal from church leadership that this ministry is valuable and life changing. Speaking of the nature of God's call to men and women in His church, Elisabeth Elliot says: "The Bible does not explain everything necessary for our intellectual satisfaction but it explains everything necessary for our obedience and hence for God's satisfaction."[2] God is not only looking for women to obey His mandates; He is equally concerned that men discharge their God-given responsibility in the local church. To neglect at least a cursory look at the kind of role God desires men to take in the church of Jesus Christ is to leave out the rest of the story. It is like trying to remove my footnotes from their place on the page only to have my computer say, "This is not a valid action for footnotes!" To portray the potential of spiritual health in a church only by calling women to embrace the holy task mandated by God in His Word and ignore the part men play is not a valid action. The spiritual health of any church is enhanced when *men and women work and serve together* to reflect the purposes of God.

Women Need Godly Men

Women need godly men as well as godly women in their lives and in the local church because none of us was meant to function independently of each other. In a well-prepared orchestra, the lead violin sets the tone for the other instruments to follow. But women need godly men in the local church because God has given qualified men the responsibility to take leadership. Those who are not in official positions of leadership are told it is a good thing to want to be (1 Timothy 3:1) and to strive to meet the qualifications given. To abdicate this leadership role is to relinquish responsibility before a holy God and to deny spiritual health to the church. Leadership in the local church is the privilege of the man who is willing to obey and speak God's truth in the context of all his relationships so he can be valued and respected.

The Model of Manhood

When you think of a man, what is the first thing that comes into your mind to define him? Why not begin with the first man, Adam. He and Eve are not only different physically from one another, but Adam's rela-

tionship with God is different from Eve's. The thing that God asks of him
that He does not ask of Eve is the fact of responsibility in representing God.
He receives instruction on how life in the garden is to work (Genesis
2:15–17). He names the animals (Genesis 2:19–20). He shares the task of
filling and subduing the earth with Eve (Genesis 1:27–30). That is why
when Eve, deceived by Satan, gives the fruit to Adam we are amazed at
his silence and his lack of responsibility. If only he had said something—*no*
would have been a good start. But he abdicates his responsibility, and you
know the rest of the story. His silence is not unlike the pride of Lucifer who,
when he is responsible to protect the holiness of God, is filled with his
own greatness and becomes the irresponsible spirit in the universe. Larry
Crabb in *The Silence of Adam* says:

> But when the serpent struck up a conversation with Eve, designed to muddle her think-
> ing about God's goodness, Adam said nothing. Yet he was listening to every word! He
> heard Eve misquote the command of God that he Adam had carefully communicated
> to her. He was watching when she began looking at the forbidden tree. He saw her
> take a step toward the tree and reach out to pluck some of its fruit. And he didn't do a
> thing or say one word to stop her. Adam remained silent! Why?[3]

Let me suggest that Adam's silence was born out of his unwillingness
to take responsibility for the situation before God. There is no doubt in
God's mind who is responsible before Him for the mess these two are now
in: "But the LORD God called to the man, 'Where are you?'" (Genesis 3:9).
God did not come calling Eve. He called Adam. It is Adam who is uniquely responsible to remember what God has said. When God finds Adam,
he admits his fear: "I heard you in the garden, and I was afraid because I
was naked; so I hid" (Genesis 3:10).

It is Adam who is responsible. He was responsible to speak to Eve what
God had said with "a confidence and wisdom that comes from listening
to God."[4] But he forgot what God had really said. He forgot God and remained silent until he was asked by God to speak up.

Real Men Speak Up

From the earliest chapters in Scripture, it seems that the clearest definition of the man who pleases God is *the man who acts in a responsible manner for what God has asked him to do*. Most models from the Old Testament
are marked with the shadows of sin lurking in their hearts. Joseph remains

consistent in his refusal to remain silent. He is not silent when he reveals God's will to his family through his dreams even though it instills hatred from his brothers (Genesis 37:5–11). In the face of temptation, Joseph resists Potiphar's wife and appeals to the holiness of God (Genesis 39:6–23). Nor is Joseph silent when he has the opportunity to bless those who meant evil to him. Because he has lived responsibly in a pagan nation, God honors Joseph and gives him opportunity to serve grander purposes in places where his brothers do not (Genesis 41–45). Why? Even as an old man, having responsibly carried out the word of God, he is able to see his place in the purposes of God (Genesis 50:19–21).

You will see a similar thread running through the life of the Lord Jesus. He speaks faithfully of the Father, responsibly doing His will (John 17:8–12). Full studies have been done on the final sayings Jesus gave from the cross where He enters into the burden of our sin. Think of some of the things He says: He asks the Father to forgive His enemies (Luke 23:34). He makes provision for His mother (John 19:26–27), promises eternal life to the undeserving thief (Luke 23:43), and declares the suffering of the cross finished (John 19:30 and Luke 23:46). His words to His men as He leaves the earth are a call to speak up and lead the church (Acts 1:6–8).

It is because of the apostles' responsible leadership that we hold in our hands the New Testament. After the Spirit was poured out on them, the disciples were faithful to their call. They bore witness to the Christ at the peril of losing their lives. It is true, they did not do it independently of the godly, obedient women added to their number. Women of great honor who had met Jesus Christ like Joanna and Susanna would be there (Luke 8:1–3). Women of great need who had met the risen Christ like Mary Magdalene were among the band (Matthew 28:1). And women with great spiritual skills of listening (Mary of Bethany), serving (Martha), helping with practical needs (Dorcas, Lydia), and teaching (Priscilla) shared in the ministry as the Holy Spirit moved. But the apostles and the elders they appointed did their leadership uniquely. They preached the gospel (Acts 2:14ff.; 7; 10:34–43). They planted churches. They taught sound doctrine (Acts 15:19–35).

They went on to communicate clearly to the second generation how the church should function even when false teachers threatened her life (Acts 13:13–15:18; Acts 16 and 17; 1 Thessalonians 2:13–20). They gave clear instructions as to the kind of men who should be elders (1 Timothy 3:1–7), emphasizing the specific conduct those in the Ephesian church should follow. They taught the premise on which the church would grow.

The Pastoral Epistles to Timothy and Titus leave no doubt as to the responsible place men have in the purpose of God. A godly man is to be valued and respected. The responsibility given to qualified men to uphold the sound doctrine of the apostles is called leadership. Leadership is influence. Leadership in the local church is the privilege of the man who is willing to obey and speak God's truth. Piper and Grudem in their discussion on the responsibility of male leadership in the church say this: "The aim of leadership is not to demonstrate the superiority of the leader, but to bring out all the strengths of people that will move them forward to the desired goal."[5]

The vibrant faith we are to remember is to be modeled in leaders who care about the spiritual health of the church more than changing the rules after the game has started. Nor have they tweaked the details to fit the culture. They have authority and, like Adam in the garden, are "men who must give an account" (Hebrews 13:17). On the basis of their responsibility, we are to consider their way of life and imitate their faith (Hebrews 13:7–8, 17).

It is important to say that men who take their spiritual responsibility to lead in the local church can look to the model of the Trinity. They see the beauty of equality of worth in the Godhead and difference in function modeled like nowhere else. They are not obligated to teach that equality in worth demands exchange in role. They accept and teach that God the Father and God the Holy Spirit did not die on the cross. They teach that the Son is no less God because He humbled Himself to the obedience of death. That the Father is no less God because He sent the Son. That the Spirit is no less God because He was sent by the Son to convict sinners and illumine truth. They understand that equality of the value and worth of each member of the Godhead is not threatened because they function differently. Their roles are not interchangeable. Nor are ours as man and woman.

This mystery of difference in function both in the Godhead and the church is both awesome and holy. We are only asked to imitate it (Ephesians 5:21–33). This mystery is not a problem for God. It should not be for us. The equality men and women celebrate is that together we share the "gracious gift of life" (1 Peter 3:7). Together we enjoy the full benefits of salvation (Galatians 3:28), and together we receive the gifts of the Spirit (1 Corinthians 12:4–6). But, as Romans 12:3–8 clearly reminds us, "These members *do not all have the same function*" (italics added). There is nothing interchangeable about Christians. There is nothing interchangeable about men and women. The mere thought ruins the mystery of what Paul teaches in Ephesians 5:21–33. We differ in gifts and abilities as well as physically.

We share God's blessings but differ in the grace given to us (Romans 12:6). But that is not a problem for God. It is His right to arrange His grace as He wishes (1 Peter 4:10).

Real Men Qualify for Leadership

In the early church when a crisis of feeding widows arose, Christian males who qualified for that leadership were "men of good reputation" (Acts 6:3 NASB), apparently chosen to be deacons. They were filled with the Holy Spirit. The male leaders in the church are not to pray publicly with their heads covered (1 Corinthians 11:4–7) but to pray out of a life of holiness (1 Timothy 2:8).

In the Pastoral Letters, when Paul instructs Timothy and Titus to appoint elders, he tells them that the elders are to be above reproach. This general characteristic includes the following: "the husband of but one wife, temperate, self-controlled, respectable, hospitable, able to teach, not given to drunkenness, not violent but gentle, not quarrelsome, not a lover of money. He must manage his own family well and see that his children obey him. . . . He must not be a recent convert" (1 Timothy 3:2–6).

The context is clear in the book of 1 Timothy: A man who takes the spiritual responsibility of his wife and children seriously has met one of the most significant qualifications for godly leadership in the local church.

Real Men Respect Others

No serious reader of the New Testament can observe the Lord Jesus' life without noting how He respected and valued women. He liberated women in ways we may not appreciate, given our culture. He spoke to women like the Samaritan woman (John 4), something no rabbi would do publicly. He allowed women who came to believe in Him to minister to Him as He went up and down Palestine (Luke 8). He shared intimate teachings with Mary (Luke 10:39) and entered into theological discussion with Martha (John 11:21-27). The respect the Lord Jesus showed women affected the apostles' teaching. Both Peter and Paul valued the women who opened their homes to house the church. Peter says when a woman models the ancient practice of a gentle and quiet spirit, her husband, though an unbeliever, may be won by this beautiful, submissive, responsive attitude (1 Peter 3:1–5). Peter says that the man who loves his wife in a considerate way, treating her with respect, keeps his prayers from being hindered (1 Peter 3:7)!

Paul highly values women who shared in the task of preaching the gospel with him—Priscilla in Acts 18 and many others whom he lists in Romans 16. Paul asks Timothy to teach the men to develop an atmosphere of protection and care in the local church. The men are to treat the older men like fathers, the younger women like sisters, and the older women like mothers in order to maintain purity (1 Timothy 5:1–2). He gives men the responsibility of authority in the home (1 Corinthians 11:3; Ephesians 5:23), and wives are to submit to the loving leadership the man brings to his marriage (Ephesians 5:22–28). The husband is commanded to love his wife (Ephesians 5:28 and Colossians 3:19), and the wife is commanded to respect her husband (Ephesians 5:33). These commands are not without purpose. They set out the men from the boys and the women from the girls, all with the purpose of providing godly leadership for the body of Christ.

Real Men Share the Load

In chapter 3, one of the important core values for the church that empowers women to serve women was *maturity among its members.* That growth usually happens because the individual men who lead see the value of partnering in the load. I work on a church staff with eleven men who grant me great honor. We celebrate the differences. We share the load. We take seriously the mandates given in 1 Timothy 2:9–15 and 5:9–10 where Paul describes the way a godly woman uses her gifts. I teach women the high privilege of the charge given in Titus 2:1–5 where Titus is commanded to teach sound doctrine so the godly older women will teach the next generation of women with an astounding reason: *"So that no one will malign the word of God."* None of the men with whom I work insist on doing the task God has called me to do. In fact, they are deliberately cautious in their relationship with younger women as Paul warns in 1 Timothy, and they take great precautions.

Women committed to becoming fully developed Christ followers in the spirit of Titus 2:3–5 hold in their hands and hearts an enormous amount of spiritual power. It is a privilege denied men. It is the power to convince a watching world that God's purposes for men and women to function together in the church reflect the glorious interdependence of the Holy Trinity. The power does not come in exchanging roles but in celebrating harmony. The power comes when women take up the task of teaching the next generation of women to know and obey God's Word (Titus 2:3–5). The spiritual power comes when women take hold of God's mandate for women in the church and get on with the job.

Real Men Take the Lead

No orchestra requires all the members to play first violin. The result would be a sound that is shrill and annoying. Rather, when the lead violin sounds the note, the different instruments follow. The results? Harmony! A blending of music that fills the concert hall, delights the maestro, and convinces the listening world there is nothing quite like it in all the earth. The church of Jesus Christ needs men who will lead holy lives. That is the tone the leaders must sound, and the rest of the church will follow. And the church needs women who will lead holy lives. That is the tone that must follow for harmony to occur. When men and women together lead holy lives, they model the Savior in leadership. They model the Savior in love. Most of all they show to the world the mystery of God wrapped up in a family called the church.

THINK ABOUT IT

Do not underestimate the spiritual effect a responsible and godly man has on his family and the local church. Do not underestimate the goal of finishing well for the glory of God. It is easy and exhilarating to begin something. It takes faithful obedience to keep your integrity before the human and spiritual family. The history of God's people is littered with those who have not finished well.

Learn from the past so the future will be secure for the people of God. Take the following people and, using the book of Acts and the Epistles, state the primary characteristics of the men and women who worked with Peter and Paul in planting and cultivating the infant church. Do this so you will be ready for those who come to your home or your class, like Priscilla with Apollos, to teach the way of the Lord more clearly (Acts 18:26).

Look up
- Acts 1:26 (Matthias),
- Acts 6:1–6 (Stephen and other deacons),
- Acts 8:26-40 (Philip),
- Acts 9 (Saul who became Paul),
- Acts 9:36–42 (Dorcas),
- Acts 11:22–26 (Barnabas),
- Acts 12:12–15 (Mary, the mother of John Mark, Rhoda),
- Acts 13:1–3 (prophets and teachers: see names),

- Acts 15 (apostles and elders, James, Silas),
- Acts 16:1 (Timothy, Lois, Eunice, cf. 2 Timothy 1:4–5).

NOTES

1. Lauren F. Winner, "The Man Behind the Megachurch," *Christianity Today*, 13 November 2000, 58.
2. Elizabeth Elliot *Discipline, the Glad Surrender* (Tarrytown, N.Y.: Revell, 1982), 43.
3. Larry Crabb, *The Silence of Adam* (Grand Rapids: Zondervan, 1995), 11.
4. Ibid., 12.
5. John Piper and Wayne Grudem, *Recovering Biblical Manhood and Womanhood: A Response to Evangelical Feminism* (Wheaton, Ill.: Crossway, 1991), 39.

MISSION, CORE VALUES, COVENANT DOCUMENTS, EVALUATIONS
WORKSHEET

DEVELOPING A WOMEN'S MINISTRIES MISSION STATEMENT

I. A Mission Statement

Whether you are a small or large church and whether you have women's ministries in your church or not, it is never a waste of time to clarify in your mind *what exactly is your mission.* You will not be required to reflect the mission statement of the hospital downtown or the contemporary club or golf club! But as women who are Christ followers in the local church, you will be responsible to obey God's Word. Your mission statement then should reflect three assumptions:

1. God's Word contains *a clear purpose* for women who are Christ followers.
2. Though God's principles *transcend* culture, they must be *integrated into all cultures.* God's Word is supraculture (above culture) and is the final authority on life and practice.
3. Since God intends the local church to be the primary womb where newborn Christ followers are cared for and brought up, you need to know the resources (spiritual gifts, skills, etc.) available to and the real needs of women in your church.

A mission statement reflects the truths the group believes about its purpose for existence.

II. Effective Mission Statements Answer Important Questions

The following questions will help you discern what your mission statement should be. Remember, you are not called to do the whole work of the church—God has given women a mandate to fit in with the church. You cannot do everything. Nor will you be able to do all things equally well. At the same time, whenever you serve women, you serve the family although your focus will be on growing healthy and godly women, what you say and do will affect those they live with.

1. WHY?
What is the main reason for our women's ministries to exist in our local church? (or at the district/regional/national level)?

2. WHAT?
What *services or ministries* will our women's ministries provide for the women in our families, the local church, our neighborhoods, and other parts of the world? What needs should we meet?

3. WHOM?
Whom *(persons or groups)* will our women's ministries serve? (See the questionnaire included at the end of this section to research your group.)
How will we address all ages, all stages of women in the church?
How will we address the women without Christ in our community?
How will we serve those whom our church sends out?

4. WHERE?
What geographical area will our women's ministries serve?

5. WHAT ELSE?
What kind of people make up our church?
What makes the women in our church unique?

III. Effective Mission Statements Include Important Statements

1. Once you have answered these questions, *include a "so what" statement* to show what you want to see happen if you follow the mission statement. Two examples follow at the end of this section to illustrate this point.

2. A mission statement explains the reason, purpose, and justification for your women's ministries group. Its primary statement is a verb.

3. Mission statements *should never be "written in stone."* (See 1 Chronicles 12:32.) Because nothing stays the same, it is important for leaders to review their mission yearly. We must be like the sons of Issachar who, because they read the times well, knew the direction they needed to go at their time in history. Renewed mission statements are born out of the *desire to remain sensitive to human needs and faithful to God's calling.*

IV. Effective Mission Statements Result from Following a Careful Strategy

Here are some practical "action points" if you and your core team are ready to write a mission statement. My suggestion is you keep your brainstorming group to a single digit, preferably three to five people who can think strategically and with vision. This always comes *after* you have researched your group and answered the five *w* questions.

1. Give out worksheets prior to the meeting (as per above) so everyone whose input you want can do their homework.

2. Consider inviting an outside facilitator who is familiar with your church's culture and the passion the core shares about women's ministries.

3. Allow "insider and outsider" thinking. By that I mean you will need to keep in mind why you have been left on the earth and not raptured to heaven! You can do a lot of spiritual socializing in heaven; now is the time for holy encounters with others.

4. Allow yourself enough time to write and rewrite; you may want to set aside a half-day or day to work on this together.

5. The goal is practicality, not perfection. You want *a working mission statement,* not one fixed in stone that says you must do everything nor one that restricts you unnecessarily. When you say too much, you will never accomplish your mission. When you say too little, you box yourself into a particular time and culture in history. Your mission statement *should be broad enough to give you freedom and narrow enough to allow you to focus on what you do best.*

6. The first result should not be etched in stone. You need one person to take the lead.

7. Allow time for brainstorming during the meeting. You need someone as a scribe.

8. Do a rough draft and step back; live with it for a week or so. Then meet again.
9. Finalize the draft and then distribute to the core.

V. Effective Mission Statements Must Be Memorable and Functional

1. Your mission statement should be *short enough to remember and long enough to make sense!* Every member of your group should know your mission statement. If you cannot remember it, it will not serve its purpose nor allow you to plan with integrity.
2. Your mission statement *should work!* You must ask regularly: "Does our women's ministries group reflect our mission statement? Is it working? Do women recognize the mission statement in who we are, what we do, whose needs we meet, where we serve, and our desired purposes?"

SAMPLE MISSION STATEMENT

MISSION STATEMENT FOR
TRINITY WOMEN'S MINISTRIES, REDLANDS, CALIFORNIA

Trinity Women's Ministries exists to
(verb—what?) **Equip** *women*
(where?) *in a safe place*
to
(verb—what?) *Learn (skill in godly living from God's Word)* (how?)
(verb—what?) *Lead (doing good works in the sphere God has placed her)* (where?)
(verb—what?) *Love (for the family, as in Titus 2:3–5)* (where, who, how?)
(verb—what?) *Look (reaching out to those who are lost at home and abroad)*
(purpose/effect on women)   ***so that***

Women are changed
The family is sheltered
A legacy is left
and
Each woman knows she is valued by God.

Trinity Women's Ministries
Trinity Evangelical Free Church, Redlands, CA 92373

TRINITY CHURCH WOMEN'S MINISTRIES
MISSION STATEMENT
(Sample)

(Purpose statement)

Women's ministries exists to

> *equip women* in this local church
> - to *learn* God's Word
> - to *lead* within their God-given spheres
> - to *love* those in their families
> - to *look* for those who need Jesus

(Strategy statement)

> *through* planned and spontaneous safe moments in Christian community *sharing fellowship, giving praise to God, studying God's Word, praying, and motivating each other to love and good works*

(Goal statement)

> *so that*
> - each woman is *changed,*
> - the family is *strengthened,*
> - the church becomes *healthy,* and *God is glorified.*

CORE VALUES FOR WOMEN'S MINISTRIES
(TRINITY CHURCH, REDLANDS, CALIFORNIA)
(Sample)

In order to stay in close partnership with the core values and mission statement of our local church, we developed this set of core values. They directly
reflect the core values of our church while staying true to the mission
statement of women's ministries. You might want to begin by doing these
four things:

1. Identify your church's core values.
2. Examine the task before you to minister to women.
3. State the main values the core group of women believe in.
4. After discussion, express them in words women in your church can
   remember.

Based on the mission statement we have adopted, Trinity Women's Ministries agrees to respect and incarnate the following core values:

We value *the study of the Bible in the context of our local church.*
- Trinity Women's Ministries focuses on God's Word.
- Our responsibility is to bring women to an understanding of God's
  Word.
- Any "role" we take is secondary to godly character, which is shaped
  by God's Word.
- Any personal growth is a result of applying God' s truth to our lives.

We value *the presence of God with us through prayer and praise.*
Women's ministries is fueled by intimacy with God more than infor-
mation about God.
- We pray because we believe God hears us and answers prayer.
- We pray as individuals, calling out to God to bless us (1 Chronicles 4:9–10).
- We pray as a three-strand cord, knowing God is with us (Matthew
  18:18–20; Ecclesiastes 4:12).
- We pray for each other, together, and praise God for what He is doing.

We adopt and obey *transferable biblical principles.*
Women's ministries is concerned about timeless principles that transform people. The biblical mandates of Scripture determine whose we
are and what we become.

- God's truths are revealed to us across centuries.
- God's truths are woven through stories within culture.
- God's truths are established through symbols to be understood and obeyed by this generation.

We encourage the *including of and serving of others.*
Women's ministries is a place where learners belong and the learned serve. We are more than a social club.
- We are aware of needs (felt and real, by young and old).
- We are concerned that outsiders are brought in (we are not exclusive) and insiders stay, ready to serve.
- We identify ministry models that work in today's world based on God's truths.
- We support those who serve in missions at home and around the world.

We value *spiritual gifts and creativity that invest for eternity.*
Women's ministries encourages the use of every spiritual gift within this local church.
- We use our gifts in the womb of the local church for the edification and common good of the body of Christ.
- We are not afraid to speak biblically with creative and pragmatic insight, insisting the expression clearly reflect God's truth and not simply artistic expression.
- We provide a safe place in the local church to equip women for living life with skill and godly poise.

We value clear purposes *to equip women to learn, lead, love, and look.*
Women's ministries seeks to respond to God's Word by equipping women to learn God's Word, lead in their God-given sphere, love their families, and look for those who don't know Jesus.
- We recruit women to a vision, not a program.
- We develop people rather than a program.
- We lead and function as a team working together—never as lone rangers (a visionary, a shepherd, and an administrator).
- We respect authority in the church and take responsibility for our behavior.
- We commit to nurture and nourish women for God's glory and their good.

We give away *grace.*

Women's Ministries functions best when individuals judge their own motives first and then give away grace to others.

- We go regularly to the cross for forgiveness and cleansing. We are known to repent.
- We gladly give away the grace of God as the stronger one coming to the aid of the weaker because the weaker cannot help herself.
- We give away grace freely to those we serve, uncritically and generously.

We are *lifestyle* **more than event oriented.**

Women's ministries values the daily expression of random acts of kindness and regular obedience.

- We practice a lifestyle of discipleship: Matthew 28:18–20, *the Great Commission* (a lifestyle of "making disciples")
- We practice a lifestyle of Christian love: John 15:12, *the Great Commandment* (a lifestyle of "loving the brothers")
- We practice a lifestyle of evangelism: Acts 1:8, *the Great Charge* (a lifestyle of "bearing witness")
- We practice a lifestyle of dependence: Ephesians 5:18, *the Great Companion* (a lifestyle of "being filled with the Spirit")
- We practice a lifestyle of godly and responsible living: Titus 2:1–5, *the Great Concern* (a lifestyle that "leaves a spiritual legacy" by investing in the next generation).

We value *generosity in serving and in giving.*

Women's ministries encourages women to practice the generous use of time, talent, and monies they possess for God's eternal purposes.

- We share generously with all within the local church.
- We share generously with those who have less than we have.
- We share generously out of our resources given to us by God.

We promise women to expect
the following at any women's ministries event:

- To be included (you belong here)
- To be protected (this is a safe place)
- To receive grace (no one here is perfect)
- To be encouraged (by God's Word and God's family)
- To be instructed in wise living (God's Word is our lifeline)
- To be mentored, nurtured, and nourished in planned as well as serendipitous ways (the older and younger together)

TRINITY WOMEN'S MINISTRIES LEADERSHIP COVENANT

Serving women in the context of a local church is not simply filling a slot. It is a holy undertaking that requires the power of the Holy Spirit to be the right person and to do the right thing. It is coming under the umbrella of the protection of godly leaders. The right to serve in a large task grows out of faithfulness proved in a small task. In order to ensure that women's ministries is "a safe place" for women of all ages and stages of life, each leader in any area should thoughtfully evaluate her motives, participation, and service as she ministers to women. The following covenant is for each woman as she joins the leadership team. It asks for a serious commitment to an important responsibility. It assumes faithfulness to the leadership team and protects the local church from division and disunity. It permits the team players to show high regard and respect of others' part in the task and allows for no surprises (criticism of plan, program, or people). All women in TWM are expected to sign the covenant before serving.

Dear Women's Ministries Team Member,

Thank you for willingly serving the Lord Jesus in women's ministries. It is a joy to have you on this team. We pray as we work together, and we will use our gifts and different leadership styles to complement each other. We care more deeply about working together as a team than any performance anyone may give. Unity and joy is the primary focus of our work together.

Because involvement in women's ministries takes time, effort, preparation, and commitment, we ask you to make this commitment on a yearly basis. The covenant below will offer you the opportunity to willingly and responsibly share in this ministry. The leadership of women's ministries will support your decision and will praise the Lord if He continues to lead you to partner with Trinity Women's Ministries.

WOMEN'S MINISTRIES COVENANT

Please read the following statements carefully and add additional comments on the back.

1. My husband and/or family strongly support my decision to serve in women's ministries/specific event: _____

2. I am personally committed to a growing and intimate relationship with the Lord Jesus Christ and am regularly spending time in the Word and in prayer.

3. I concur wholeheartedly with the doctrinal statement of Trinity Church and am an active, supportive participant.

4. I concur wholeheartedly with the core values and mission statement of Trinity Women's Ministries.

5. I will faithfully prepare what is needed so I can carry out my service with godly grace.

6. I will hold each team member in high regard. I will speak well and not ill of them to others. I will speak with honesty and grace to them about concerns that involve them.

7. I will be sensitive with regard to confidential information.

8. I will show a humble, teachable spirit and dress with modesty.

Signed _____ Date _____

PERSONAL WOMEN'S MINISTRIES QUESTIONNAIRE
(Sample for initial evaluation)

1. What are the three strengths of your local church women's ministries?
   a.
   b.
   c.

2. What two things could your local church's women's ministries do better?
   a.
   b.

3. What do you consider the most important characteristic of someone who would mentor you?

4. Where in your local church can you find this kind of woman?

5. What is the greatest need of older women in your local church?

6. How does your local church's women's ministries address this need?

7. What is the greatest need of younger women in your local church?

8. How does your local church's women's ministries address this need?

9. What is the greatest need of single women in your local church? Of married women?
   a.
   b.

10. How does your church address these needs?

11. Name another woman/women with whom you can confidentially pray about these requests. Covenant to pray with her/them and as the answers come, list them below!

Answer _____ Date _____

Answer _____ Date _____

Answer _____ Date _____

Evaluation of Workshop
Workshop Leader: _____
Workshop:_____

An unexamined life is not worth living! Evaluation with the director, ministry coordinator, or oneself is useful for several reasons.

- It allows the one who evaluates to express appreciation, encourage, and instruct the one evaluated in strengths and weaknesses.
- It allows the one evaluated to appreciate and maximize her strengths and to better recognize and manage her weaknesses.
- It provides time to reflect on the usefulness of the seminar/workshop and whether the leader is in the right "niche" using her spiritual gifts.
- It provides a graceful way to bow out and re-enter.
- It offers the evaluated one opportunity to sharpen her/his skills.

Name_____ Phone _____
Please mark each factor S (satisfactory), NI (needs improvement), or O (outstanding)

General Remarks
1. Workshop began promptly and time was used well. _____
2. Leader welcomed easily and built relational bridge with group. _____
3. Leader set positive tone. _____
4. Workshop focused on God's honor and valued His priority. _____

Leadership and Group Dynamics
1. Leader was well prepared. _____
2. Leader used partner to advantage and/or props made sense. _____
3. Leader answered questions clearly. _____
4. Leader manifested creativity. _____

Subject Matter _____
1. Participant gained new perspective on topic. _____
2. Participant found subject matter applicable for personal ministry. _____
3. Participant was satisfied with biblical subject matter. _____
4. Participant received practical tools to use in her local church. _____

Other Comments:
1. What you liked best._____
2. What you would change._____

EVALUATION FOR SMALL GROUP LEADERS
(Sample)

An unexamined life is not worth living! Evaluation of any ministry coordinator, including a small group leader, is useful for all involved. It enables
those who seek to lead to sharpen their skills and realize whether or not
they are serving the Lord in the right place.

Use the following evaluation at the end of one full semester of service.
Discuss each factor on the basis of these ratings: S (satisfactory), NI (needs
improvement), or O (outstanding).

Name _____ Phone _____

Meeting Time/Place _____ Number in Group _____

_____

General Tone
_____ 1. Begins promptly.
_____ 2. Opening remarks.
_____ 3. Welcomes easily, builds relational bridges.
_____ 4. Sets positive tone.
_____ 5. Noticeable features, extras, etc.

Leadership
_____ 1. Leader is well prepared.
_____ 2. Leader facilitates discussion smoothly, manages study well.
_____ 3. Leader is prepared beyond required work, questions.
_____ 4. Leader deals well with awkward situations.
_____ 5. Leader exhibits the ability to teach.
_____ 6. Leader manifests creativity in leading.

Group Dynamics
_____ 1. Members relate well to each other.
_____ 2. Members model care for each other outside group time.
_____ 3. Members prepare study.
_____ 4. Members participate in discussion.

Prayer Time

_____ 1. Leader is transparent.

_____ 2. Group shares openly.

_____ 3. Group focuses well on prayer.

Leader's Evaluation of Self and Group

_____ 1. I have bonded with this group.

_____ 2. Group size has grown ____, stayed the same _____,
grown smaller _____.

_____ 3. Individuals have grown in their walk with Christ because

_____

_____

_____ 4. This is a good "niche" for _____
because _____

_____

General impressions and suggestions for improvement:

BIBLIOGRAPHY

Burke, H. Dale. *Different by Design*. Chicago: Moody, 2000.

Clouse, Bonnidell and Robert G. *Women in Ministry: Four Views*. Downers Grove, Ill.: InterVarsity, 1989.

Crabb, Larry. *The Silence of Adam*. Grand Rapids: Zondervan, 1995.

Elliot, Elisabeth. *The Mark of a Man*. Old Tappan, N.J.: Revell, 1981.

———. *Let Me Be a Woman*. Wheaton, Ill.: Tyndale, 1999.

———. *The Shaping of a Christian Family*. Nashville: Thomas Nelson, 1992.

Farrar, Mary. *Choices*. Sisters, Oreg.: Multnomah, 1994.

Hunter, Brenda. *In the Company of Women*. Sisters, Oreg.: Multnomah, 1994.

Inrig, Gary. *Life in His Body*. Wheaton, Ill.: Harold Shaw, 1975.

———. *Quality Friendship: The Risks and Rewards*. Chicago: Moody, 1981.

Kent, Carol. *Becoming a Woman of Influence*. Colorado Springs: NavPress, 1999.

Mayhall, Carol. *From the Heart of a Woman*. Colorado Springs: NavPress, 1976.

Nair, Ken. *Discovering the Mind of a Woman*. Nashville: Thomas Nelson, 1995.

Otto, Donna. *The Gentle Art of Mentoring*. Eugene, Oregon: Harvest House, 1997.

Roberts, Cokie. *We Are Our Mothers' Daughters*. New York: Quill, 2000.

Saucy, Robert and Judith TenElshof, ed. *Women and Men in Ministry.* Chicago: Moody, 2001.

Stanley, Paul and Clinton, J. Robert. *Connecting: The Mentoring Relationships You Need to Succeed in Life.* Colorado Springs: NavPress, 1992.

Wilkinson, Bruce. *The Prayer of Jabez.* Sisters, Oreg.: Multnomah, 2000.

Moody Press, a ministry of Moody Bible Institute,
is designed for education, evangelization, and edification.
If we may assist you in knowing more about Christ
and the Christian life, please write us without obligation:
Moody Press, c/o MLM, Chicago, Illinois 60610.